In His Image

In His Image

A Workbook on Scriptural Holiness

Allan Coppedge & William Ury

THE BARNABAS FOUNDATION

PROVIDENCE HOUSE PUBLISHERS
Franklin, Tennessee

Printed in the United States of America

14   13   12   11   10   2   3   4   5

Library of Congress Catalog Card Number: 00-104177

ISBN: 1-57736-191-1

Cover design by Gary Bozeman

All Scripture quotations are taken from THE HOLY BIBLE, Revised Standard Version. Copyright 1971, Division of Christian Education of the National Council of the Churches of Christ in the United States of America.

PROVIDENCE HOUSE PUBLISHERS
238 Seaboard Lane • Franklin, Tennessee 37067
800-321-5692
www.providencehouse.com

Contents

How To Use This Workbook

For over twenty years the Barnabas Foundation has been crafting Bible studies to distill the key concepts from the Word of God every disciple ought to know. Over the next several weeks we would like to provide you with some foundational studies of the holy life.

Jesus is the model for all holy living. From the New Testament we have tried to extract the major lessons He tried to build into His disciples. Next we set them in a contemporary context so we may apply them to our lives and help others do the same. Our focus in this workbook will be trying to understand what Jesus has said to us through His Word and through the model of His discipleship training of the twelve. Out of this context we will then assist each other in attempting to apply these key principles to our lives and ministries.

This workbook is designed for twelve weeks of involvement. This should fit appropriately into a semester study for those on campus or for a quarter of activities within a local church calendar.

While the design of the workbook is to give you sufficient material to study during a certain time frame, you will not want to be bound by the calendar. Oftentimes it will be necessary to lengthen the period of time to study any one subject. For example, it may be necessary to take two weeks on a study from the workbook, especially if you are using it for a group study. If this needs to be done, then by all means feel free to do it.

If you are studying the workbook as a group, it may also be necessary to interrupt the series of studies because of special needs in the group. If it is necessary for your group to focus on a particular urgent issue facing you, then your leadership may wish to develop a Bible study from the Word to meet that need and take as many weeks as necessary to do so. You can then feel free to return to your sequence in this workbook.

The key issue here is that this workbook is a tool, not a master! It is designed to serve you, not to be a taskmaster. You will want to use it to help you, and lay it aside when the Spirit indicates it is time for an interruption.

When used in a group, each member is asked to prepare the study before the group meeting. This will mean a careful working through of the materials that help you focus upon the Word of God and its implications for your life as a disciple of Jesus. Of course, a leader must be more prepared than anyone else!

If for some unavoidable reason a member of the group is not able to complete their preparation before the group meets, by all means encourage them to come to the group meeting. However, significant sharing should come out of serious time in the Word of God and seeing its implications for theirs and others' lives. So if someone has not had time to complete their study preparation, you may wish to suggest that they be less of an active participant for the study time. They should fully participate in every other part of the group meeting.

At the end of each lesson you will find a list of passages for additional study. These provide other evidence to support the conclusions of the lesson. It may be that they can serve as the Word portion of your devotional time. Study, prayer, and meditation over these passages will certainly strengthen the spiritual lives of disciples in the truths and experience that these studies are designed to promote.

One final word about using these studies in a group. You will find the Spirit is able to use your time together most effectively when you come prepared to your group meeting in the following ways: 1) With your study done and with your Bible and study materials in hand; 2) Praying for each member of the group and their receptivity to the Lord as the group meets; 3) Praying and expecting God to speak to you as you meet together with the group.

Preface

In every age there are some who aspire to have an intimate relationship with a holy God and to the godly life that results from such a relationship. But with this longing there also come questions about the means to develop this relationship. How do we know God like this? How do we cultivate the deepest possible relationship with Him? How do we let Him make us like Himself?

As God begins to make Himself known in the earliest chapters of scripture, one factor that unfolds is the possibility of real intimacy with Him. Several key Biblical characters model this for us. Adam, Enoch, Noah, and Abraham, for example, know God well, walk with Him, and have fellowship with Him. One of the earliest roles of God that appears in scripture is that of friendship. He is available to know people and cultivate relationships, person to person, friend to friend.

This close relationship with people was one of God's two major purposes at creation. One purpose was to know and have fellowship with us, and the other was that we would be like Him. To accomplish these purposes He made us in His own image. Two significant parts of this image are personhood and character. Since we reflect His personhood, we are made for personal relationships. The triune God is a social being and so are we! We are made for relationships, first with Him, and then with other believers. We are also made to reflect His character. This character He describes early in scripture as "holy." Not surprisingly, then, He calls His people to choose to be like Himself: "Be ye holy for I am holy" (Lev. 11:44–45; cf. 1 Peter 1:15–16).

How do we respond to these two needs: to be in close relationship with the holy God and to reflect His nature? God has answered our questions in His Word. He begins with His revelation in the Old Testament and then brings this revelation to another level in the New. Under the new covenant the coming of Jesus and the coming of the Holy Spirit give us the fullest picture of who God is and what we are to be like. In the Gospels and Acts we get this fuller understanding of who this holy God is and how we are to relate to Him; He is like Jesus, and we relate to Him like the disciples did with Jesus!

Knowing Jesus is the secret of knowing the Father. Knowing Jesus is also the way to know the Holy Spirit! The Father and the Spirit are both like Jesus, and knowing one is the way to knowing the other two. It is out of these relationships with a triune God that He begins to shape those following Him. He has His ways to make disciples like Himself, holy as He is holy, i.e., like Jesus.

It is with these two things, knowing the triune God and reflecting His likeness, that these studies are concerned. What are the biblical passages that help us focus on these two goals? How do we work through them? How are they connected? This set of Bible studies is designed to deal with these questions.

Several of these studies were originally written to assist people in learning to be serious disciples of Jesus. They were produced by the Barnabas Foundation, a discipleship training organization, to help disciples see what Jesus has for them as they follow Him. They were first used in the discipleship training manual called *Loving Jesus: A Guidebook to Mature Discipleship.* The Barnabas Foundation has produced several guidebooks to help disciples in their spiritual journey. The first one is *Knowing Jesus* and is about God's purposes for His disciples. The second one, entitled *Following Jesus,* is about the means of how to be a disciple of Jesus. The fourth of these guidebooks is called *Serving Jesus,* and it is about learning to make other disciples and serving in ministry to other people.

Loving Jesus is designed to help disciples go on to a mature stage of discipleship in their preparation to make other disciples. Two essential things in the New Testament seem especially important in order to be ready to be a disciple maker. One is receiving all that Jesus offers in terms of holiness of heart and life and the fullness of the Holy Spirit. The second is an understanding of spiritual gifts and how these relate to our ministry to other people. So *Loving Jesus* focuses on these two things: holy living and spiritual gifts.

We have extracted the set of studies on holiness and the Holy Spirit and expanded these in this separate format as a workbook on scriptural holiness. This gives room for more than twice as many studies in this area and allows it to be used separate from the discipleship training series.

In His Image is designed for personal Bible study on these subjects. It also may be used for group study, as was its original design in *Loving Jesus*. If used in a group, we strongly recommend each member spend about two hours in Bible study on each lesson as preparation before coming to the group to share. This way all participants do some serious study of the scripture to hear from God, and then they are able to share insights about His Word when they meet together.

The Bible studies are interactive. You will need a standard translation of scripture (we use the RSV). We have given you some background and observation on each passage studied. We will then be asking you some interpretive questions and providing some interaction with you on matters of interpretation. This will be followed by some application questions that speak of the implications of what you are finding for your own life. After certain key interpretative questions, we will provide some discussion of meaningful answers. Like other adult education materials, we will try to give you feedback as you go along. That means, of course, that it's possible to "run ahead" and look for the answer. But that is not the purpose of these studies and will quickly short-circuit your own learning curve. We challenge you to answer each question as best you can, and then check your answer and expand it with comments that we may add. It takes discipline to do this, but that is what learning is all about!

We hope you will find these Bible studies a helpful encouragement to you on your own spiritual journey. If we at the Barnabas Foundation can be of any further help to you as you seek after God and attempt to follow Him as His disciple, please feel free to call on us.

Setting the Pace

John the Baptist models a standard for ministry

QUICKENING YOUR THINKING

1. What do you suppose was the influence of John and Jesus on each other as young men before they began their ministries?

_____

_____

2. What would you think were the greatest influences of John's life and ministry on others?

_____

_____

GETTING PERSPECTIVE

Certain figures in scripture tend to slip by without all the attention they deserve. They come at times and places where they are overshadowed by others of larger stature and so sometimes go unnoticed. Such is the case with John the Baptist. Because he comes as a part of God's plan to introduce Jesus, he is often treated as only part of the introduction!

Yet, Jesus said that among those born of women, there was none greater than John the Baptist (Luke 7:28). A reasonably high compliment coming from the Son of God! A careful reading of the Gospels suggests that John's ministry set the stage for much of what was to come throughout the rest of the early church. It may well be that God not only raised John up to introduce Jesus, but also used him to exemplify certain principles for ministry and certain theological emphases that were to continue through the whole New Testament. Accordingly, we invite you to explore with us the life of this incredibly influential man of God.

By way of introduction we will focus on the godly heritage from which John came and the implications of this for his own life. We will then look at four key dimensions of his ministry and observe how these set a pattern for the rest of the New Testament. In the next study we will see how John models in his own life an experience of the fullness of the Holy Spirit and how the character he exhibits under the full control of the Spirit sets the standard for godliness in the early church.

◆ A GODLY HERITAGE
Turn in your Bible to Luke 1:5–25, 39–45, 57–80 and read carefully.

✣ JOHN'S PARENTS

Godliness produces godliness, so it should not surprise us that when we find a godly man, we discover a godly heritage behind him.

1. What are the key things said about the character of John's parents in Luke 1:5–7?

_____

_____

This is a couple committed to the Word of God. They are walking in full obedience to the Word, and the righteousness of God is so obviously working in their lives that their conduct and attitudes can be described as being "without blame."

2. What evidence do you find throughout this chapter that they are people of deep personal faith and prayer?

Zechariah:

_____

_____

Elizabeth:

_____

_____

3. What is the relationship of each to the Holy Spirit?

_____

_____

4 What happens as a result of their relationship to the Holy Spirit? What are the implications of this?

_____

_____

5. What three characteristics of John's home would you like to see evident in your family?

_____

_____

While the data is not extensive about this couple, it is full enough to give us a picture of a godly couple, seeking to follow after God, full of the Spirit of God, whom God wants to use in a special way. It is not an accident that He has chosen these two, who are walking by faith and available to His Spirit, to raise John, who will become the leader of a great spiritual movement.

✣ GOD'S PLAN

It is clear from reading the gospel story that God brings John into the world at a unique time for a special mission (John 1:5–6). There has not been a spiritual movement in Israel for many years, and God is going to use John to begin a great revival. He brings him into a certain family, at a certain time and in a certain place. In His sovereign choices, God has raised up John to play a crucial role with his life.

What is specifically stated about the early life of John in Luke 1?

_____

_____

There is no question that God has some special work for John to do and is getting him ready for that ministry. John is a classic example of God's choosing a man for His work based on God's own foreknowledge of John's choices. God is not forcing John to follow Him or be available for His service. Rather, God, foreknowing that John is going to choose to follow Him and be available, picks this man to accomplish some very significant things at the beginning the New Testament era.

◆ CHARACTERISTICS OF JOHN'S MINISTRY

God gets His man ready for service. God's first step is the godly heritage of John's own home. Then John apparently spent some time seeking God alone in the wilderness (Luke 1:80). We do not know how long this period of time was, but it certainly was a time of listening to God and getting to know Him intimately.

A third factor in John's preparation for ministry may have been a relationship with Jesus. These two men were cousins. While John lived in Judea and Jesus in Galilee, it is certainly possible they had contact during their teens and early adulthood. There is silence over these years, but with their close family connections (suggested by Mary's relationship to Elizabeth) it is very possible these two had time to talk, dream, pray, and seek God together.

While it appears that John did not know that Jesus was the Messiah until God revealed that to him at the beginning of Jesus' ministry (John 1:31), it is certainly possible that they had some time together as young men, and may well have shaped each other's thinking about certain aspects of ministry.

We are going to find that several dimensions of John's ministry also show up in Jesus' ministry. How much they learned from each other is not clear, but it is likely they reinforced each other with regard to these parallel aspects of ministry that God blessed in both of their lives.

It is significant that the four dimensions of John's ministry that will be the focus of our attention also show up in the life of Jesus and in the experience of the early church. The implication is that these ought to be accents in the life of everyone seeking to be in ministry for God. Not everyone will have the same spiritual gift orientation that John did or be called to exactly the same work. At the same time there are some crucial characteristics of his ministry that are valuable for people with different gifts, different callings, and living at different times.

These four major characteristics of John's ministry are (a) his commitment to ministry based on the Word of God; (b) his evangelistic call for repentance and forgiveness; (c) his making of disciples; and (d) his preparing new believers for the baptism of the Holy Spirit. Let's investigate each one of these in some detail.

1. A MINISTRY BASED ON THE WORD OF GOD

▲ In the Ministry of John
Turn in your Bible to Luke 3:1–20 and read carefully.

1. How does the Word of God (in the Old Testament) provide a foundation for John's understanding of himself and his ministry?

_____

_____

Not only is John's life and ministry based upon the written Word of God, he is God's vehicle for reception of a direct word from the Lord to him.

2. How is this described?

_____

_____

John is functioning in the same way as the Old Testament prophets did, namely, as the mouthpiece of God. He receives God's revelation and proclaims God's Word to God's people. God has already spoken through the Old Testament. Now He begins to speak in a fresh way, and John is the first installment of the Word of God that is going to become the New Testament.

▲ *In the Ministry of Jesus*
Read Matt. 4:12–17, 5–7; and Acts 2:16–28.

1. In Matthew 4:12–17 the gospel introduces Jesus' ministry. What role does the Word of God have in this introduction?

_____

_____

2. When Jesus begins to give His disciples the content of the New Covenant (Matt. 5–7), He shares with them the basis upon which He is building His teaching (Matt. 5:17–19). What does Jesus say about the role of the Word of God ("the Law and the Prophets") for His disciples?

_____

_____

_____

_____

3. At the end of Jesus' first teaching of the disciples (the Sermon on the Mount) He talks about the role that His own words will play for disciples. What does He say about His own teaching and how does He expect disciples to respond (Matt. 7:21–29)?

_____

_____

_____

_____

Like John, Jesus begins His ministry by opening to people the written Word of God. He adds to this the direct revelation of God through Him. As the Living Word of God, He begins to place His words and teaching on a par with that of the Word already given (Matt. 7:24–29).

▲ In the Early Church

Not surprisingly, then, when the Spirit of God comes on the day of Pentecost, Peter stands up to preach and his proclamation is based on the Word of God. Citing a passage from Joel 2, Peter uses the Word to explain what has happened on the day of Pentecost and to invite people to respond to Jesus by calling upon Him in faith. While he begins with Joel, he also quotes the Psalms as the Word of God. His preaching is a proclamation that is founded upon the Word of God as given in the Old Testament and the Living Word of God that has recently been among them in the person of Jesus. Peter's words, of course, themselves become part of the Word of God in the New Testament.

This focus upon God's revelation as the basis of how people ought to respond to Him is characteristic of all the rest of the New Testament. The foundation for the new church and for all ministry is first the Word of God given in the Old Testament, then His Word given through John, Jesus, and the apostles.

The accent upon ministry founded upon the Word of God must not be lost. If we are going to follow in the steps of those like John, Jesus, Peter, and others in the New Testament, then we, too, must also take seriously the Word of God given in the Old and New Testaments. This must become the foundation for understanding what kind of ministry needs to be done, what the content of our proclamation ought to be, and the specific direction for ministry as we seek to serve God.

Building ministry upon the Word of God presupposes an understanding of the Word of God. That means we cannot do as John and Jesus did without serious study of the Word of God. Searching the scriptures and then using them as a basis for life and ministry will be absolutely indispensable for us if we are to imitate their example.

Are you willing to make a definite commitment to build your life and service for Jesus on the Word of God?

_____

_____

✢ AN EVANGELISTIC MINISTRY

▲ In the Ministry of John
Focus on Luke 3 and Mark 1:1–8.

1. What are the indicators that John has an evangelistic ministry? What is he calling people to?

_____

_____

2. What are the results?

_____

_____

3. What kind of change does John expect in the lives of those responding to his ministry?

_____

_____

John's challenge is for people to repent, i.e., to turn away from sin and things that are keeping them from God. This turnaround in their lives must be accompanied by a confession of sin, implying a godly sorrow. People receive the promise that God will forgive their sins and heal their hearts. The use of baptism seems to be a public declaration of turning to God and away from sin, as well as a declaration of their faith that God has forgiven them.

The repentance that John accents in his preaching is a transforming repentance. It is not merely emotional sorrow over sins or over the consequences of sin. Rather, it involves the deliberate change in one's life by turning away from sin and turning to that which is right. Luke tells us that John's charge to people who are responding to his message is that they need a clear evidence of fruits of repentance in their lives. Those who have two coats are to sell one and share with the less fortunate. The tax collectors are exhorted only to receive what is their legal due. Soldiers are charged not to intimidate people or rob them, and to be content with their wages. These come as representative examples of character that is committed to righteousness and of those who are trusting God to provide any additional needs that they may have. In other words, John is calling for a kind of repentance that expresses itself in concrete actions and personal relationships. He is looking for people to turn to God in such a way that it has incredible ethical consequences for their lives. It is definitely a call to righteousness in personal living (Luke 3:8–14).

4. How is John's evangelistic activity related to his call to "prepare the way of the Lord"?

_____

_____

_____

John is preparing the way of the Lord by helping people to get their hearts right before God so they might believe in Jesus when He does appear. This does not mean there has been no element of faith already in their personal experience with God. Certainly the turning away from sin, confession to God, and looking for a changed life in Him involve a significant degree of faith. They believe God can and wants to do something new for them, and they are already committing themselves to take steps to allow God to do that.

Yet, this step of faith in God is just the beginning. It is like a "warm up" to get them ready for trusting in Jesus and all the further changes He desires to bring in their lives.

This means that John's ministry is characterized by an evangelism that calls people to open their hearts to God by repentance, confession, receiving God's forgiveness, and a public declaration of this faith in Him.

▲ In the Ministry of Jesus
Read Mark 1:14–15, 2:1–22; Luke 24:47; Acts 2:38.

1. When Jesus begins to preach, He follows the same pattern. What is His first call to people (Mark 1:14–15)?

_____

_____

_____

2. Jesus is concerned about forgiveness of sins (Mark 2:1–22), and He is likewise looking for people who will publicly declare their allegiance to Him (Mark 2:13–15). When He gets ready to send out the disciples at the end of His time with them, what is His charge to them (Luke 24:47)?

_____

_____

▲ *In the Early Church*

The disciples not only hear Jesus, they observe His model and recognize that this emphasis in evangelism was to be a central part of their own ministry. Accordingly, when the Holy Spirit comes upon the disciples on the day of Pentecost, Peter, speaking for the others, begins to preach the gospel about Jesus. When some ask what they are to do, Peter's response is, "Repent and be baptized every one of you in the name of Jesus Christ for the forgiveness of your sins" (Acts 2:38). This call to repentance, forgiveness, faith in Jesus, and public confession of that faith in baptism becomes a characteristic mark of the early church. They have a heart to see people come to know God, trust their lives into His hands, and receive the saving grace that Jesus had made available. It is an evangelistic concern of the entire New Testament and of the Christian church at its best times throughout its history. It is the pattern of ministry God wants for His people in every age, and it begins in the New Testament with John the Baptist.

If there is going to be a revival of biblical Christianity in our own day, we will have to return again to this biblical model. Evangelism is not an optional extra for the church of Jesus nor is it only for serious disciples. It is a central part of who He made us to be. One of the questions for us is, "Are we a part of an evangelistic church that is seeing men and women come to saving faith in the Lord Jesus?" A second question is more personal. "Are we praying and seeking opportunities to share our faith in Jesus so that others may come to know Him in a personal way?" Is this an area that needs a revived emphasis in your own life and service for God?

_____

_____

_____

✣ THE MAKING OF DISCIPLES

▲ *In the Ministry of John*

Turn in your Bible to John 1:29–42 and read carefully.

John is certainly not only interested in people making initial decisions, he is interested in their becoming in-depth followers after God. Therefore, he chooses some of those who are responding to his message of repentance, confession, and faith, and he begins to invest in them as his disciples.

1. Two disciples of John are introduced to Jesus. Who is the one named? Can you guess who the writer is referring to as the other disciple?

_____

_____

2. Make a list of all the characteristics of these two in this passage (John 1:35–42):

_____

_____

_____

_____

_____

One of those who responds to John the Baptist's preaching and attaches himself as a disciple is Andrew. It seems very likely that the other person introduced in John 1 is the writer of the gospel, the apostle John (John 1:35, 37). These two men want to learn and grow, as evidenced by their following John's direction when he points them to Jesus. They definitely have hungry and teachable hearts, and they are anxious to receive all that God has for them. They want something more than just the experience of repentance and faith. They are looking for a deeper relationship with God and with those following after Him.

3. What title did those following John give him (John 3:26)?

_____

_____

4. What was the significance of this in the first century?

_____

_____

They call him "Rabbi" after the custom of the day for a group of students following a teacher (John 3:26). The experience involves significant learning and transference of the life of the rabbi to his students. While this whole phenomenon of disciple-making takes on another dimension in the life of Jesus, it begins with John's investment in some of those who are responding to the spiritual revival under his ministry.

This means that the first New Testament disciple maker is John the Baptist. He sets the tone for all that is to come.

▲ In the Ministry of Jesus

1. What in this passage (John 1:29–42) indicates that Jesus followed John the Baptist's pattern for this method of ministry?

_____

_____

_____

_____

2. Does this ministry of making disciples come at the beginning, middle, or end of Jesus' ministry?

_____

3. What is the significance of this?

_____

Jesus picks up this pattern as soon as He begins His ministry (Mark 1:16–20). All four gospels indicate that as a part of His early deliberate strategy for ministry, He begins to draw disciples around Himself and invest His life in them. They continue with Him throughout all His public ministry, and then become the core of those who are sent forth to make other disciples.

▲ In the Early Church
Read Acts 2:41–47.

1. All the disciples learn their lessons well from Jesus. After the tremendous response of people to Peter's preaching on the day of Pentecost, what do the disciples begin to do for the new believers?

_____

_____

_____

2. Where did the twelve get these basic spiritual habit patterns?

_____

This pattern of discipleship shows up in the fruits of their training efforts in people like Barnabas, who then passes them on to Paul, who in turn invests in people like Timothy, who is then charged with continuing to disciple others (2 Tim. 2:2).

This whole chain of disciple-making that is so characteristic of New Testament Christianity begins with John the Baptist. Apparently, God intends for all future believers in Christ to understand that there is more than the experience of God's saving grace. There is a life of learning if one is to be a follower after Jesus as His disciple. It requires disciple makers to invest themselves in others, and to train them in the same way John and Jesus trained their disciples.

If we are going to be a faithful part of New Testament Christianity, then we must return again to this biblical pattern. When Jesus sends forth the twelve to fulfill the Great Commission, He is not just thinking about missionary activity. He is thinking about the creating of disciples in all parts of the world, but the focus is upon "making disciples." The questions for us are, "Are we doing that in our lives?" "Are we following the pattern John sets and Jesus follows in making disciples for God?"

3. What is Jesus saying to you about this in your own life?

_____

_____

✦ A MINISTRY OF PREPARING DISCIPLES FOR THE BAPTISM OF THE HOLY SPIRIT

▲ In the Ministry of John
Return to John 1
The last aspect of John's ministry that gets repeated attention is his focus on the coming of the Holy Spirit.

1. How is this promise described in John 1?

_____

_____

All four gospels note that when John introduces Jesus, he makes the promise that Jesus is the One who will baptize believers with the Holy Spirit (e.g., John 1:32–33). John is looking forward to the coming of the Spirit in His fullness on the day of Pentecost. He has the incredible privilege of not only introducing the second member of the Trinity in the person of Jesus, but also the third person of the Trinity in the Holy Spirit. John does not want disciples to be caught off guard. There is a Trinitarian emphasis in all of his preaching. He desires people to come to know the Father through the Son and then be prepared for what the Father and Son will do in their lives through the Holy Spirit.

This promise of the baptism of the Holy Spirit is the only promise repeated in the New Testament six different times. Five times the promise comes from the mouth of John the Baptist (Matt. 3:11, Mark 1:8, Luke 3:16, John 1:32–33, Acts 11:16). One time it comes as a promise from Jesus (Acts 1:5).

2. What are the implications of this repetition?

_____

_____

John, of course, is anticipating the day when the disciples of Jesus will be filled with the Spirit of God on the day of Pentecost. He does not live to see that day, but he does enjoy the experience of the Holy Spirit himself. He longs to see that other disciples know the fullness of the Spirit of God in their lives. John knows how valuable God's Spirit working through him is for his own ministry, and he covets this for the character, thinking, and ministry of every future believer in Jesus.

▲ In the Ministry of Jesus
Read Luke 24:49 and Acts 1:4.

1. How does Jesus reinforce this same promise of the Spirit for His disciples?

_____

_____

Jesus has the same focus. When He comes to the end of His own ministry, He charges His disciples not to leave Jerusalem until they receive the promise of the Father. This is the experience of the baptism of the Spirit that Jesus desires for disciples to have in order for Him to finish His work in their lives and to enable them to go about the ministry to which they have been assigned. What John first introduces, Jesus explains in more detail. He commands His disciples not to begin making other disciples until they have received this Holy Spirit in His fullness.

▲ In the Early Church
Read Acts 8:14–17.

The disciples not only heard Jesus and received the Spirit for themselves at Pentecost, but they learned the lesson that every follower of Jesus needs the same experience in their lives.

1. When Peter and John are sent down to encourage the new believers in Samaria, what is the apostles' first concern on arriving?

_____

_____

2. What do they do to see that the Samaritans take advantage of the promise from John and Jesus?

_____

_____

They lay their hands on these new Christians, pray for them, and the Spirit comes on that group just as He did on the 120 at Pentecost.

This seems to be the pattern God desires for everyone. God wants to draw believers to Himself that He might have full control of them when the Spirit fills them completely. This is not to say the Spirit is not in the life of every believer. When a person believes in Jesus, he gets access to the Father, and the Spirit begins to work in his life. There is no dividing the Trinity. When you get one member, you get all three!

At the same time it is certainly possible for people to have a close relationship with Jesus, like the disciples did, and still not be under His absolute control. That is where the experience of the fullness of the Spirit of Jesus becomes so significant. The Lord wants His disciples, and all future disciples, to come to the place where they not only know Him, but they are fully committed to Him with a whole heart just as He is to the Father. This is what Jesus would like to see in every one of us. He wants us to experience the fullness of His Spirit, and let that become a crucial part of our relationship to the Triune God and our ministry to other people.

✤ REVIEWING JOHN'S MINISTRY

John is the leader of an incredible spiritual revival in Israel. God is blessing what he is doing to touch the spiritual lives of hundreds of people. When Jesus starts His own ministry, He does not start from scratch. He enters into a revival movement that begins under John. What John is doing is absolutely essential for the ministry of Jesus as well as that of the early church.

1. Summarize in your own words the four major characteristics of John's ministry:

_____

_____

_____

_____

2. Is one of these foundational for all the others?

_____

3. If one of these is foundational for the others, is there any logical order to them? How would they build upon each other?

_____

_____

_____

_____

If the Word of God includes God's direction for how we are to serve Him, then it is not surprising His Word becomes the basis upon which we do everything else. Here is where John (and everyone following his footsteps) learns what is important to God. This should lead to an understanding that God desires people to come into a right relationship with Himself, and this implies for us a ministry of evangelism. Evangelism starts the process of getting the spiritual lives of people rightly related to God, but then it should lead to a deepening of that relationship through discipleship. After walking as a disciple of Jesus for a period of time, then comes the promise of the fullness of the Spirit of Jesus upon the lives of those who are following Him.

4. Are all four of these characteristics of John's ministry also a part of your own life and service for God?

_____

5. If not, which area(s) will need a new commitment on your part for God to use your life in the way He used John and many others throughout the New Testament?

_____

_____

Are you willing to ask God to give you a heart for making all four of these areas a part of the way He uses you to touch other people for Him? If so, this is the place to take some time in prayer and make a fresh commitment to each one of these four things and let the Spirit guide you as to how God wants to begin to accent each one in a new way in your ministry to others.

Prayer Suggestion

Lord, what must I do in each of these areas so that they can become characteristic of my life and service for You? Open my eyes to see the concrete steps I must take to let You build these into my life.

Memory Verses
Mark 1:4 and 1:8

Additional Passages for Study

You may wish to study some of these passages more fully during the Word portion of your devotional time.

1. Isaiah 40:1–11.
When a voice is "to cry in the wilderness," what are the things God is about to do? Make a list.

2. Matthew 3:1–12.
What are the symbols connected with John in 3:4 and who do they point to? Check 2 Kings 1:5–8. What parallels do you see between these two prophets?

3. John 1:19–28
How does the description of John in this passage introduce Jesus?

4. Mark 1:14–22.
Which of the characteristics of John's life show up in the beginning of Jesus' ministry?

Illustrating the Goal

John the Baptist models a standard of godly character

QUICKENING YOUR THINKING

1. Can you think of anyone in the Old Testament who is fully controlled by the Spirit of God?

_____

_____

2. What do you think would characterize a contemporary person who was fully controlled by God's Spirit?

_____

_____

_____

_____

JOHN'S ROLE

John understands his own function in God's plan as the one who introduces Jesus. He is the voice of one crying in the wilderness, "Prepare the way of the Lord!" All of his ministry helps to get ready for the coming of Jesus. He does this in a variety of ways. As the leader of an incredible spiritual revival in Israel, John is helping quicken people to spiritual things. Hearts are turning away from sin and to God. There is a new awareness that God desires to work among His people. Many are now sensing the time may be close when God is ready to send His Messiah to fulfill His long awaited promises. There is excitement in the air, and John is humanly responsible for this spark of revival among God's people.

John also prepares the way for Jesus by modeling the kinds of ministry that are going to be necessary to touch people for God. In our last study we highlighted the four things that John emphasizes and others in the New Testament emulate. John "set the pace" by establishing a standard of:

—A ministry based on the Word of God.

—An evangelistic call to repentance and forgiveness.

—Making of disciples.

—The promise of the baptism of the Holy Spirit.

An additional way in which John helps prepare the way of the Lord is by modeling a godly character, something that we will see even more clearly in the person of Jesus. Godliness is introduced in the life of John, and it comes in terms of what the Spirit does to make people like God. We will see that John himself is described as one who is filled with the Spirit, and this prepares the way for understanding the coming of the Spirit on Jesus. In both cases the outworking of this experience is particularly illustrated in character issues. A review of what it means to be filled with the Spirit in John's life will prepare us for understanding something of what it looks like in Jesus and then later in His disciples.

◆ A LIFE MODEL: WHAT IT MEANS TO BE FILLED WITH THE HOLY SPIRIT

One of the reasons John is so concerned that others be filled with the Spirit is because of the powerful difference it made in his own life. He knows firsthand what it means to have the Spirit of God in full control of his life. It is from this state of living in the fullness of God's presence that all his ministry comes.

The description of when John is filled with the Spirit is a good reminder that God is not confined to only one way of working. What are we told in Luke 1:15 about the unusual way in which John is filled with the Holy Spirit?

_____

_____

He is the only person in scripture who is described as being filled with the Spirit of God even before his birth. The circumstances are certainly unique and unlike any other person who is filled with the Spirit in the New Testament.

The picture of John's infilling in this way comes in the midst of the story of the Spirit's filling of several individuals in Luke 1–2. Perhaps it should not surprise us that when the second person of the Trinity is coming into the world, there is also an accent on the work of all three Persons of the Trinity. Accordingly, several persons are depicted in the story as being filled with the Spirit of God, and John is one of these.

Our immediate questions are about John's volitional involvement in allowing the Spirit to fill him. Obviously, in his mother's womb he was not exercising the normal human capacities to make that experience a choice. Because of the way God works and how we see the Spirit moving elsewhere in scripture, we assume this unusual filling of John was connected with two things.

First, it is confirmed in his own life as an adult when he has the capacity to make choices. There is no evidence in scripture that God arbitrarily chooses people against their will. Rather, it is the Spirit drawing people to Himself that makes it possible for Him to work when people choose to respond positively. We presuppose, then, that John, at some time in his teens or early manhood, not only responds in faith to God but also responds with a completeness of commitment that allows God to continue to dwell in him through His Spirit in this full way.

Second, we know that God may occasionally choose to do something for a person in the light of His foreknowledge of their choices. God's filling of John in his mother's womb is best understood in the light of God's foreknowing John would choose, not only to believe in Him, but to fully surrender himself to the whole work of God through the Holy Spirit. God's choice of John is based on God's foreknowledge of John's choices of God!

With these two assumptions, we want to focus our attention, not so much on the unusual way in which John is filled with the Spirit, but on the expressions of the Spirit's fullness in his own life. Even if we had not been told explicitly that John had been filled with the Spirit, there are evidences in his life that indicate that God has full control of his life, his thinking, his relationships, and his character. We now want to look at these evidences of being filled with God's Spirit.

✣ The First Evidence Is the Holiness of John's Character

Turn in your Bible to Mark 6:14–29 and read carefully.

1. As you look for evidence of holiness in John's character, consider the following: What is Herod's evaluation of John's character?

_____

_____

_____

2. What are the implications of Herod's identifying Jesus with John?

_____

_____

_____

3. Does John's confrontation of Herod tell us anything about character (John's, Herod's, or God's)?

_____

_____

_____

_____

The clearest evidence of the godliness of John's character comes in the testimony about him from Herod. Herod believes John to be a "righteous and holy man" (Mark 6:20), and thus the king has a remarkable respect for John. When your enemy gives witness to the godliness of your character, you can be sure that it is evident to all.

A confirming word of witness comes when Herod recognizes the uniqueness of Jesus, and believes that He is John the Baptist raised from the dead (Mark 6:14). There is something about the life of Jesus that reminds Herod of John. The reason for that is the fact that John's character reflects the character of a holy God and therefore looks very much like Jesus. Even before Jesus starts His own ministry, there is a "Christ-likeness" about John that even unbelievers recognize.

The righteousness of John's life is also seen in his willingness to stand for what is right, even when that means confronting the king with the truth the king did not want to hear. John's calling Herod to account over his marriage to his brother Philip's wife is a clear evidence of John's stand on the Word of God for that which is right (Mark 6:17–18). It is a commitment to holiness as righteousness that is a part of who he is. It is the same character He desires to see in others, including the king.

So the first evidence of the fullness of the Holy Spirit in John's life is a holiness of character. This gets a special accent in its expression of righteousness in his own life and a call to righteousness in the lives of others.

❖ The Second Evidence Is a Willingness to Confront Sin and Evil
Turn to Luke 3.

What evidence do you find of a holy boldness in John that is willing to confront sin and evil?

_____

_____

_____

John is certainly very straightforward in his preaching of truth. "You brood of vipers! Who warned you to flee that wrath to come?" (Luke 3:7). It is a direct spiritual challenge designed to puncture any spiritual complacency or illusion. When people begin to respond, he has concrete suggestions of how their response of repentance and faith may be expressed in the fruits of godly character. John does not mind telling it like it is!

Not only is he willing to preach to the multitudes, he is also willing to confront the king. By pointing out Herod's sin and calling it to the attention of all Israel, he is certainly taking his life in his own hands. But because he is committed to righteousness and is a man of integrity, he is going to preach God's truth, and he will do so without distinction to all hearers. Everyone, from the king to the slave, needs to hear from God and respond to Him. This is the kind of holy boldness that comes from being under the full control of God's Spirit.

❖ The Third Evidence Is a Deep Humility
Turn in your Bible to John 1:19–34 and read carefully.

What is the evidence for a sense of humility in John?

_____

_____

_____

_____

When some are sent to inquire of John as to who he is, he rejects claims that he is the Messiah, Elijah, or the prophet expected from the Old Testament (John 1:19–21). He is unwilling to claim to be something he is not, reflecting not only humility, but also a tremendous sense of integrity. He could have refused to answer their questions, leading them to believe he could be the Messiah. He could have justified this on the grounds that the crowd might listen better if there is the possibility that he could be the Promised One. But he does not do this. He has incredible reverence for God, and therefore he is walking in integrity about his own identity, as well as about the message he has come to proclaim.

There is also in John a deep sense of unworthiness. He declares that he is not worthy to stoop down and untie the thong on the Messiah's sandal (John 1:26–27). Tying and untying of sandals is clearly the work of a servant. John sees himself in this role, and perhaps not even worthy enough to do this for the coming Messiah.

A further indication of John's deep humility is his desire to give all the credit to God for whatever happens through his life and ministry. When some want him to step forward and claim his rightful position as leader of the spiritual revival, John reminds them that he does not have anything that has not been given to him from heaven. God is the one who is responsible for what he has done, and John wants everybody to know that what is happening is due to God's activity, not his own effort (John 3:27).

✢ The Fourth Evidence Is Not Protecting His Own Position
Turn to John 3:25–30

What is the evidence that John is not selfishly guarding his own place as leader of a spiritual movement?

_____

_____

_____

When some of John's own disciples are complaining that Jesus is getting more attention than John, John has to respond in Jesus' defense. There is no question that John has been the spiritual leader of the revival movement up to this point. But now that Jesus has come on the scene, John is willing for attention to be shifted to Jesus and away from himself. He does not protect his own position as leader of a great spiritual revival. John makes the principle clear with his powerful statement, "He must increase, I must decrease" (John 3:30). This reflects not only an incredible spiritual maturity, but also a surrender of his status to God. It is a level of spirituality that only comes when one is fully controlled by the Holy Spirit.

✢ The Fifth Evidence Is an Enabling for Ministry

1. From the passages already examined, what significant fruit do you see in John's ministry?

_____

_____

_____

2. What evidence do you find in John's ministry of miracles, healings, signs, prophetic predictions, or casting out of demons?

_____

_____

3. What are the implications of this for others doing ministry "in the Spirit"?

_____

_____

There clearly is an anointing power of God on John for the ministry he is called upon to exercise. This power of the Spirit is particularly seen in His evangelistic ministry, where people are drawn into a relationship with God through a repentance and confession that leads to a transformation in their lives. This anointing is also worked out in ongoing investment in the lives of the disciples that John makes. Both the evangelistic ministry and the discipleship training are a part of the whole spiritual movement of revival that is taking place within the life of Israel.

It is significant that John's ministry is producing vital spiritual fruit but there is no mention in His work of miracles, healings, signs, or casting out of demons. The indication is that all the central things can happen in the spiritual lives of people through a ministry in the Spirit without these external indicators.

✛ THE SIXTH EVIDENCE IS A WILLINGNESS TO DIE

What evidence have you seen in Mark 6 and Luke 3 that John is willing to die if necessary to fulfill his ministry?

_____

_____

_____

A key indicator of John's living under the fullness of God's Spirit is that he has come to the place where he values God's will for him more than he values his own life. He has anticipated Jesus' later challenge to disciples, "If any man would come after Me, let him deny himself and take up his cross and follow Me" (Matt. 16:24). John is willing to deny himself, and take up his cross, i.e., be willing to give his own life if that is what God asks. To be fully submissive to the whole will of God is more important than to live!

In the ancient world when one publicly rebukes the king, he knows he takes his life in his own hands. John not only does that in public but in private with Herod. Herod, knowing John is a godly man, hears him gladly even though he is disturbed by John's preaching. Herod has resolved to protect John, but in the moment of a rash promise, he ends up giving John's head to Herodias' daughter (Mark 6:19–29).

John does not know when death is coming. But he knows that as soon as he crosses an absolute ruler, his stand for God could cost him his life. He counts the cost, and he makes his decision. Because he is fully submitted to the whole will of God, this means he is willing to speak God's Word whatever the cost. In this case, the cost is his life.

Thus, willingness to die is a significant sign that one has arrived at the place of not having his own way but fully seeking the will of God through His Spirit. It involves a death to self-will and a surrender of self-centeredness that only comes when one is fully yielded to the whole will of God through the Holy Spirit.

His willingness to do all that God asks, in spite of the cost, is one more reflection of John's Christ-like character. Like Jesus, he is willing to submit to God's will even if this costs him his life. Like the character of a holy God, self-sacrifice is a central factor of his being. Being full of the Holy Spirit has made him like the God whose Spirit controls him.

✛ THE LAST EVIDENCE IS A WILLINGNESS TO FULLY OBEY JESUS
Turn to Matthew 3:13–17.

What indication do you see of John's willingness to fully obey?

_____

_____

John's willingness to die is closely tied up with his full submission to the will of God in every area. We see this in John at Jesus' baptism (Matt. 3:14–15). Jesus comes asking to be baptized by John, and John does not want to do it. Sensing his own unworthiness in the light of Jesus' worthiness, John claims he needs to be baptized by Jesus.

John knows Jesus does not have the sin in His life that is the normal prerequisite for baptism. But Jesus is not coming to confess sin in baptism. He is identifying with fallen humanity. John does not fully understand this, and so naturally objects. When Jesus insists that he do it, John is willing to submit to Jesus' judgment, even though he does not totally comprehend the way God is working.

It is this willingness to fully submit to the whole will of God in every thing, whether we understand what God is doing or not, that is one of the marks of the fullness of the Spirit. It is not a question of the suspension of reason or common sense, but it is a submission of those faculties to God's reason, even when we cannot fully comprehend what He is doing in our lives. God is looking for total consecration, and He finds it in John. The question for us is, "Does He have the same complete submission in our lives?"

✤ REVIEWING THE MATTER

Summarize in short statements the seven evidences of the fullness of the Spirit in the life of John the Baptist?

_____

_____

_____

_____

_____

_____

Even if we had not been told that John was filled with the Spirit, the evidence of his life is that he is absolutely God's man. We see God in full control of his life in which he reflects the character of a holy God time after time. This is what the fullness of the Holy Spirit is all about, being so full of God's holy nature that one reflects godliness. John gives us evidence of what this looks like in the lives of those who are coming into this experience.

Interestingly enough, John is setting the pattern for those to follow. His life is very much like Jesus' life. Jesus also receives the fullness of the Spirit at His baptism (Luke 3:22; 4:1) and demonstrates all these qualities in His own life that were first seen in John. Later Jesus sends disciples to Jerusalem to wait for the fullness of the Spirit, and when they come out of the upper room, the disciples also have these godly qualities. What God does for John, He demonstrates fully in the life of Jesus and then reproduces again in the lives of disciples. It is the experience of being wholly God's, so we might be fully like Him. This is what God wants, and this is what John models.

As you come to the end of this study, this model will surely come with a challenge to your own heart. You may well have seen some characteristics of John's ministry that you want to be characteristic of your own ministry. What about the enabling power of the Spirit to make this ministry a reality? Has the Spirit come fully in your life, so that you might do the kinds of work for God that John did?

More pointedly, God not only wants to work in what you do for Him, but He wants to work in your character. He wants your life to reflect His likeness, holy as He is holy. The only way to do this is to demonstrate His righteous character in humility, giving God all the credit, being willing to decrease while others increase. This character comes when we surrender our will to the whole will of God and become willing to obey Jesus in whatever He asks. It is this full submission, this willingness to die for Jesus, that is a part of the total consecration necessary for the Spirit to come in His fullness in any life. But with the surrender of the will, and therefore the life, God can take a whole life and do with it as He pleases. This is His desire for every one of us.

Ask God to indicate which of these characteristics of John are not true in your own life. Then ask Him to begin to show you how they can become a reality in you.

Memory Verses
John 1:7 and John 3:30

Additional Passages for Study

You may wish to study some of these passages more fully during the Word portion of your devotional time.

1. John 1:1–18.
How is the role of John described? How is he like Jesus?

2. John 3:25–30.
How does John picture his own responsibility? Are there any additional terms/figures used about John than those in 1:19–34? What is their significance?

3. John 3:31–36.
Make a list of all the things John says about Jesus. This will give you the content of his witness.

4. Luke 7:18–25
How does Jesus respond to John's questions when John is under the pressure of imprisonment in a dungeon? How does Jesus describe John?

5. Matthew 14:1–13.
What is Jesus' response to the death of John? What do you suppose He felt at this news? How has John once more "set the pace" for Jesus?

The Holy Spirit in the Life of Jesus

Modeling our spiritual lives after the pattern of Jesus

QUICKENING YOUR THINKING

1. After the infancy narratives in Matthew and Luke, what are the Gospel stories which appear between the return of Jesus' family to Nazareth and His first public acts of ministry? Without looking, see how many you can remember.

_____

_____

_____

2. What is the one statement that every Gospel records which John the Baptist makes about Jesus' relationship to the Holy Spirit and the believer?

_____

_____

◆ THE CONTEXT FOR THE BAPTISM OF JESUS
Turn in your Bible to Matt. 3:1–17 and read carefully.

1. What kind of preaching is taking place and by whom is it being spoken?

_____

_____

2. Who is being affected by the ministry of John the Baptist?

_____

3. What do you think is the difference between John the Baptist and the other religious leaders?

_____

_____

4. Where does Jesus go to be baptized?

_____

5. Why?

_____

_____

The context for this significant inauguration of the ministry of the Messiah is deeply spiritual. The longing of Israel for redemption from its enemies, the return to the land which God had given them, and the opportunity to live the life which God had desired for them to live are all reasons for looking for the dynamic of God's presence in this new and vital revival led by John the Baptist.

◆ THE MEANING OF THE BAPTISM OF JESUS

There has been a tremendous debate about the meaning of baptism over the centuries. Some make it a work which merits or ensures salvation, others have made it so symbolic that it loses almost all of its sacramental value.

In Israel the mode of baptism is never the focus. But it is true that in second-Temple Judaism (first century Judea) those who sought to convert to Judaism were required to enter a *mikvot* or a cistern-like hole. They were to immerse themselves fully so as to symbolize death to their old way of life and to arise from another stairway to newness of life under the law. The Essenes, a rigorous religious sect, also practiced a similar ritual.

John the Baptist, using means understandable to the typical Jew and God-fearer, opened up a new and dynamic revival of baptism as a symbol of repentance. Baptism in Israel's famous river of redemption and promise carried with it high hopes of the return of the Messiah.

1. Why do you think Jesus underwent baptism if there was no need for Him to repent?

_____

_____

2. There may be a hint in the phrase Jesus uses in response to the reservation John shows in baptizing him, "it is fitting for us to fulfill all righteousness." What do you think it means in this context?

_____

_____

The baptism of Jesus was a witness to the spiritual renewal going on prior to His arrival. The Spirit of God was already at work in preparing for the ministry which was to come. True repentance only comes through the work of the Holy Spirit, and it is clear that John is uniquely endowed with the Spirit of God (Luke 1:15).

◆ THE HOLY SPIRIT AND JESUS

There is something else at work here besides the initiatory emphases of new life. There is more than simply a beginning. For as soon as Jesus is baptized and comes out of the water (Luke adds that Jesus was praying), some remarkable things happen. List them below.

_____

_____

You will of course have noticed that the strong affirmation here at the beginning of the Lord's ministry is a Trinitarian statement. This is a statement that has to do with the being/essence of God. This means we are given a glimpse into the inner life of the triune God as it is revealed in the incarnation.

Again, what do you think would be the reason for Jesus and His own Spirit to be seen in this new way, since it is very clear that the Persons of the eternal Trinity are never "separated" or "distanced"?

_____

_____

_____

Here baptism is an evidence that the life which Jesus lived was never His alone. To be a divine Person is to live life in total dependence upon another. You cannot have one Person of the Christian Trinity alone. They are Three in One. So that Jesus makes it clear from the beginning of His ministry onward—His life is not of Himself. It is given from the Father and through the Holy Spirit. Read the following verses, indicate what you find about Jesus in each, and summarize what you find in a short paragraph.

John 3:34_____

_____

John 4:34_____

_____

John 6:26_____

_____

John 6:57_____

_____

John 7:16_____

_____

Summary

_____

_____

_____

_____

The Gospels are telling us in different ways that, as George MacDonald put it, Jesus never thought of being original. His life, will, words, works, teaching, glory, and purpose— were in another. Even His redemptive ministry began with an unmistakable connection with the other two Persons of the blessed Trinity.

With the Spirit and the Father's clear witness to the fact that the Son of His Love was well-pleasing, the ministry of Jesus begins. Not with fanfare but with intimacy, not a flurry of activity but with an intensity of love. We have being before doing. Love before obedience.

Read Matt. 4:1; Luke 4:1, 14, 18.
What are we to understand about the daily living of Jesus as He ministered?

_____

What key terms are used to describe Jesus' relationship to the Holy Spirit?

_____

_____

Besides the beautiful ideas which surround the inner Trinitarian life as revealed to us in the incarnation, there is something else this context emphasizes. Life in the Spirit is not just life *of* another, it is life *for* others.

Remember that Jesus is being baptized by and with those for whom He will give His life in service, in love, and eventually in His own death. When the Spirit comes upon the Son, the shadow of the cross also passes over the scene. Everywhere the Spirit is working, it is for the redemption of another—even when that Spirit is descending upon the Son of the Father.

◆ HOLINESS, THE HOLY SPIRIT, AND THE DISCIPLE OF JESUS

1. Many things are taught us about the Spirit, but there is only one phrase which is repeated in the four gospels about what Jesus came to offer all of His followers. What do you think it is?

_____

2. What do you think, given our study above, this may mean in comparison with the life of the Savior? List your insights below.

_____

_____

There is a lot of misunderstanding in the church regarding the baptism of the Holy Spirit. There is a danger that extreme interpretations might take away the central core of its meaning which is most clearly evidenced in the life of Jesus himself.

It is instructive that the very next thing which transpires after the glory of the descent of the Spirit as a dove is an entrance into intense "hiddenness." Forty days with no preaching or healing—only fasting, prayer, and time alone with the Father and the Spirit. Discipline within the context of intimacy. This is followed by temptation and the radical trust and obedience of the Son in the face of the things to which every living person before that day had succumbed (Luke 4:1–14). He is then rejected by His own hometown for claiming to be more than they thought He could ever be (Luke 4:16–30). And then He goes to Capernaum, to invest in the lives of a group of twelve, while He carries on His public ministry (Luke 4:31–5:11). This may just be an historical outline, or it could be more.

As we take the next few weeks to look into the life of the Spirit in the heart of the believer, let us not forget the witness borne to us in the beginning of the Gospel of Jesus Christ. Before the word "repent" or a single miracle occurs, Jesus is anointed with power from on high. He does not experience much of what we would call the glamorous or the fantastic. There is no wind, fire, or speaking in tongues when the Spirit comes. If these were in any way essential to experiencing the Holy Spirit, they certainly would have been present in Jesus' life. What He does, however, redeems the world. The baptism of the Spirit models for future disciples the intimate presence of the whole Godhead that controls and enables a person to give his life for the redemption of others.

Are you willing to let the Spirit of Jesus show you who you are?

_____

Are you willing to let the Spirit of Jesus show you of Whom you are?

_____

Are you willing to let the Spirit of Jesus show you for Whom you are to pour out your life?

_____

If there is never to be the "glamorous" or the "fantastic" as we often interpret the spirit-filled life, would that be all right with you?

_____

Here is some food for thought. Take a look at the end of Matthew's Gospel in closing and read the Great Commission (Matt. 28:19–20) once more. **What new things does it say to you after a study of the beginning of the Gospel? What does "baptizing them in the name of the Father, Son, and Holy Spirit," possibly mean now besides simply leading someone to Christ?**

_____

_____

Prayer Suggestion

Ask Jesus to give you insight over the next several Bible studies as to how you might have the same intimacy with the Father and the Holy Spirit that He did.

Memory Verses
Luke 4:1 and Luke 11:13

Additional Passages for Study

You may wish to study some of these passages more fully during the Word portion of your devotional time.

1. Luke 4:1–14.
What are the key elements in Jesus' dealing with temptation? What are the implications of what He models for us?

2. Luke 4:14–44.
How is the Spirit practically related to Jesus' ministry?

3. Luke 11:5–13.
What is Jesus trying to teach disciples about the Holy Spirit in this passage?

4. Luke 24:49 and Acts 1:4–5.
What is the promise of the Father? Why does Jesus not let His disciples start their public ministry on their own without this?

The Holy One of God

Jesus sets the standard and models the concept

QUICKENING YOUR THINKING

1. If you heard someone unknown to you described as a "holy man," what would that description bring to mind? What would a holy man look like?

_____

_____

_____

_____

2. In John 6:66–69 Peter uses a specific title for Jesus. Why do you think he did this, and what is its significance?

_____

_____

_____

_____

◆ JESUS SETS THE STANDARD
Turn to Matthew 4:17–5:20 and read carefully.

✧ THE PURPOSES OF JESUS

As disciples are initially connected with Jesus, five major objectives begin to emerge early in their time together. Jesus is calling people into (1) a *relationship with Himself* (Matt. 4:19–20), so that He might work fully in their lives. This close relationship with Himself is also related to learning to live (2) *in close relationships with a few others* who desire to be disciples of Jesus (Matt. 4:18–22). It is in the context of these relationships that Jesus begins to (3) shape their *character* (Matt. 5:3–12). In order to deepen their relationships as well as affect their character Jesus begins to redirect (4) their *thinking* so that they are able to develop the mind of God (Matt. 5:17–18). Then it is out of these relationships (with Jesus and other disciples) and out of what He is doing to mold their being (their character and thinking) that Jesus is able to (5) prepare them for *ministry* to other people (Matt. 4:23; 5:13–16). For more detail on these purposes of Jesus for His disciples see *Knowing Jesus: the Guidebook to Mature Discipleship* (Coppedge and Ury, The Barnabas Foundation, Wilmore, Ky., 1998).

Jesus identifies five areas where He has some purpose/objective for His disciples. Where in this passage do you see each of them? List the reference and a one sentence summary of each area.

1. Relationship with Jesus

_____

_____

2. Relationships with other disciples

_____

_____

3. Character issues

_____

_____

4. Thinking (Ideas)

_____

_____

5. Ministry to others

_____

_____

You will notice that two of these purposes have to do with *relationships* (one's relationship to Jesus and one's relationships to other disciples); two of them have to do with the disciple's *being* (character and thinking); and one of them with *doing* (ministry). Note these categories well. Everything else that Jesus does with and for disciples is related to one of these areas.

✤ **THE CONTEXT FOR UNDERSTANDING JESUS' STANDARD**

▲ *The Background for Knowing How People Would Understand Jesus*

1. In Matthew 5:17ff, what is the authority to which Jesus appeals?

_____

_____

2. How does He expect the disciples to relate to the Word of God in the Old Testament?

_____

_____

3. In this context (5:17–48), is Jesus describing the Law (Torah) of God as ceremonial law or moral law?

_____

4. Of the five areas identified above in which Jesus has purposes for disciples, which one gets the accent in the next section (5:20–48)?

_____

▲ _Understanding Jesus' Thinking From the Word of God_

If the Old Testament is the background for understanding the character which Jesus wants to "fill full" of meaning, then some understanding of the character that God wants for His people must be highlighted from the Old Testament (i.e., the Law and the Prophets). Let's look at a couple of representative passages that help set the context for Jesus' teaching and purposes for His disciples.

Turn in your Bible to Leviticus 11:44–45.

1. What is the essential character God desires to see in His people?

_____

2. Why does He desire this character?

_____

_____

_____

Now turn to Exodus 19–20.

3. How is the same character that God desires in His people described in 19:5–6?

_____

_____

_____

God summarizes what He wants to see in His people in an introductory form in 19:5–6. Then He begins to spell out in detail what a holy people would look like in chapter 20. Here He gives to His people the ten words, better known to us as the Ten Commandments. They are really ten principles which God gives to His people to live as a holy people.

4. What is the significance of the first commandment (Exod. 20:3) for being a holy people?

_____

_____

_____

_____

5. Does this principle have to do with relationships, being, or doing?

_____

_____

If the first commandment is that God's people are to have no other gods before Him, then obviously God is looking for an exclusive relationship between Himself and His people. To be a holy people means to make God first and not worship any other gods besides Him. So the first issue for being a holy people is a right relationship with God that involves an exclusive and total commitment to Him.

This relationship principle is then followed in the second commandment (Exod. 20:4–6) by a discussion of character questions. From the Hebrews' point of view, character comes out of relationships. A right relationship with God makes it possible for Him to produce a certain character in His people. Without the proper relationship, there is no way He can reproduce His character in His people.

God is looking for a holy people and when He describes what they ought to look like, He gives a standard of righteousness (Exod. 20:1–17). This standard of righteousness tells God's people what right living will look like, and therefore, how they are to reflect His righteousness. It means that a holy God is reflecting His holiness to His people in terms of righteousness. The character of a holy God revealed in righteousness might be diagrammed like this:

Look at Exodus 20:6. What is another expression of a holy God towards His people?

_____

_____

God is not only looking for people to be obedient to Him, but He wants the relationship to be characterized by love. He describes His commitment to His people in terms of "steadfast love." The Hebrew word *hesid* may be translated loving kindness (NASB), unfailing love (NIV), steadfast love (RSV), and occasionally kindness or mercy. It clearly is a strong word for love that includes commitment.

The two major expressions of God's holiness may be shown in the following graph.

What response is God looking for from a holy people in these two areas of righteousness and love (Exod. 20:6)?

_____

_____

The responses of a holy people might be understood in this way.

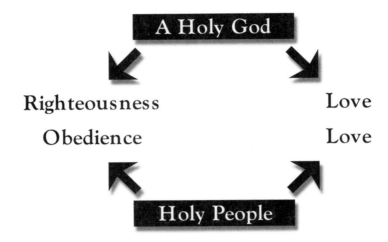

A holy people relate to a holy God by responding to His standard of righteousness with obedience and responding to His love with love. These are the cornerstones of a right relationship with Him.

If a holy people reflect the holiness of God toward other people, how would their holiness parallel the holiness of God?

_____

_____

If a holy people look like a holy God, then this ought to be expressed in relationship to others in terms of righteous living and loving hearts. The whole picture looks like this:

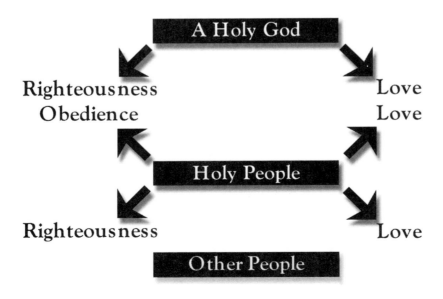

It is this picture of a holy God and how a holy people are to relate to Him in obedience and love, and then how a holy people express God's holiness in terms of righteous living and love towards others that sets the proper context for understanding Jesus' desire for holy character in His disciples.

✣ THE KIND OF DISCIPLES FOR WHICH JESUS IS LOOKING
Return to Matthew 4 and 5.

▲ The Priority of a Relationship
If Jesus is looking for disciples in a manner that parallels what God was looking for in a holy people in the Old Testament, how should the disciples' relationships to Jesus (Matt. 4:18–22) parallel the first commandment?

_____

_____

_____

_____

▲ Relationships and Character
Jesus now begins to describe for the disciples the character He wants to see come out of their relationship to Him. What are the two main parts of the character He describes in 5:20–48?

_____

_____

If the Old Testament is Jesus' pattern (5:17), then righteousness and love are a reflection of what basic character concept?

_____

Does this imply that when Jesus is calling His disciples around Him (to be the new Israel of God) that He is looking for the same character in them that God was looking for under the Old Covenant?

_____

Even though the word "holy" does not appear in these two chapters, it is apparent that the content of holiness is certainly expressed. The Old Testament gives us a picture of a holy God who is looking for a holy people and this holy God expresses His character in righteousness and love. This seems to be the very same character Jesus is looking for in disciples. If they are walking in righteousness (5:20–42) and expressing the same love of God towards others (5:43–48), then it would strongly imply that Jesus is looking for exactly the same character in His disciples that God has always looked for in His people (Exod. 19:6). **Further, if the character God is looking for is a reflection of His own character in people, then what does this tell us about the constancy of God's character throughout both Testaments? You may want to check 1 Peter 1:15–16.**

_____

_____

_____

_____

▲ Character: Holiness as Righteousness
How does Jesus fill righteousness with a fuller meaning in this specific example (5:21–26)?

_____

_____

_____

_____

In this section (5:20–42) Jesus is clearly giving some representative examples of righteous living. He talks about the standard of righteousness in relation to the standard of righteousness that God has already given under the Old Covenant. He clearly did not address every issue of righteousness or every commandment. This is not an exhaustive statement about righteous living but a representative statement of how to take God's standard from the Old Covenant and find its fullest and deepest meaning.

Jesus is looking for a holy character that is reflected in righteous living towards other people, but He is certainly looking for a holiness/righteousness that is not just external. He wants not only right outward behavior, but a holiness/righteousness that comes from the inward being of the heart. It is the internalization of godly character that He desires to see in His disciples.

▲ Character: Holiness as Love
Look at the second expression of holy character in 5:43–48. What part of this character is Jesus presupposing the disciples will do and what part of current understanding in His day is He correcting?

_____

_____

_____

_____

When Jesus exhorts disciples to love their enemies, He certainly is not asking them to do something easy! It is not difficult to love friends, acquaintances, or others who respond positively to us, but Jesus is looking for more than this. How is this possible? Notice how He describes this in parallel to the love of a heavenly Father. How is this love Jesus desires to see in His disciples like the love of the heavenly Father?

_____

_____

_____

_____

In this context, what does Jesus mean by being "perfect as your heavenly Father is perfect" (v. 48)?

_____

_____

_____

Jesus is certainly looking for disciples who reflect the loving heart of God. Apparently, it is not very difficult to love those who love you back, but Jesus is looking for disciples who love people whether they are loved in return or not. This is an unconditional, self-giving love like the love of the Father. This passage is key for understanding why some in the Christian church have described a serious walk with God as "Christian perfection." This phrase conjures up different connotations for different people, but if this passage were the context for deciding its content, to what would "perfectness" refer?

_____

_____

Given this context, would "Christian perfection," "biblical perfection," "perfectness," or "perfect love" be an adequate description of one part of the holy character Jesus desires to see in His disciples?

_____

_____

✛ How Do You Get There?

▲ *Always a Future Goal or a Realizable Possibility?*

Jesus has given us a standard as to what holy people ought to look like. But how do we get there? In our fallen human state this is not a natural way to live! Even those beginning as serious disciples of Jesus, who have repented of their sins and have believed in the gospel, do not start out looking like this standard. Is there any realistic hope for this in the lives of disciples? Is this a realizable possibility in terms of character or is this "pie in the sky" which will never be achieved in this world?

It may be that we have some clues as to how one might begin to experience this kind of godly living in Matthew 6. The suggestions come in the middle of the Lord's prayer.

Turn to this prayer in Matthew 6:9–19 and read it carefully.

▲ *A Holy Name*

You will remember that the third commandment (Exod. 20:7) has to do with taking the "name" of God in vain. This does not have to do with swearing as much as it has to do with identifying oneself with the name or nature of God. "Name" in the Old Testament was identified with a person's nature or character, so the name of God is most often described with the adjective "holy." Usually it is the "holy name" of God which describes the essence of His being. Taking the name of God in vain under the Old Covenant meant identifying oneself as one of the people attached to a holy God without reflecting the holiness of God's character.

Now as Jesus begins to teach His disciples to pray, He has them say, "hallowed be thy name" (6:9). "Hallowed" is an old English word meaning to "make holy" or "sanctify." To hallow God's name means to *acknowledge* the holiness of His name/nature or *express* the holiness of God's nature. We both acknowledge Him and express His nature in holy character. This is the standard which Jesus is trying to set before disciples, but how is this possible? The key seems to come in verse ten.

▲ *The Kingship of God*

When Jesus begins to talk about the "kingdom" of God, the term really means "kingship" (*basileia*). When the disciples are charged to pray for the kingship of God to come, what are they really praying for? How is the coming kingship of God defined in this passage?

_____

_____

_____

_____

It is clear that the definition of kingly reign in the lives of disciples has to do with God's will being done in their lives. The key has to do with their submission to the will of God. What part of this will of God are they to do and how often? What is the significance of the phrase "on earth as it is in heaven"?

_____

_____

_____

_____

In teaching the disciples how to pray, Jesus seems to have included a segment about how they may come under God's kingly rule and therefore reflect His name. The key is total submission to the full will of God. This means God's perfect will is done in the lives of the disciples "on earth," just like God's will is done perfectly "in heaven." To be doing the perfect will of God must imply, then, a total submission of the disciple's will to the whole will of God.

How is this concept of full submission to God's kingly rule and His total will in one's life a parallel to the first commandment (Exod. 20:3)?

_____

_____

_____

_____

◆ JESUS MODELS THE CONCEPT
Open to Luke 3:21–5:17, a passage that parallels the beginning of Jesus' ministry we have seen in Matthew. Read carefully 3:21–22, 4:1.

✛ JESUS AND THE TRIUNE GOD

The story of the baptism of Jesus opens the picture of His life and public ministry. It is a tremendous Trinitarian passage in which the first and third Persons of the Trinity introduce the second. Each of the four Gospel writers record this story because of its significance, so it introduces many things about Jesus and what He desires to do. We will not exhaust this passage and its significance, but let's look at some key ingredients for the purpose of our study.

What adjective highlights the nature of this Triune God?

_____

There are many other descriptions of the nature and character of God. He could have been described as loving, just, or merciful. Why were not one or more of these other adjectives used in connection with His name?

_____

_____

What is Jesus' relationship with the Holy Spirit?

_____

_____

_____

What terms describe what happens here between Jesus and the Spirit? What is the resulting relationship?

_____

_____

What is Jesus' relationship with the first Person of the Trinity? How is it described?

_____

_____

What is there about Jesus (that God knows or foreknows) that pleases the Father?

_____

_____

_____

_____

Jesus has just been baptized by John. This was not because of sin in His life, like everyone else who needs baptism. Rather it was to identify Himself with sinful humanity. This story comes as a clear reminder that Jesus is the Son of Man as well as the Son of God. Luke has already made the case in chapters 1 and 2 for the supernatural nature of Jesus' birth and, therefore, His blameless character. Now Luke wants to indicate that Jesus is beginning His ministry, not only in His divinity, but also in His humanity. Jesus then comes as a unique model of what God is (in His divinity) and what people ought to be (in His humanity).

Immediately after the baptism, the Spirit of God descends upon Jesus. Again, this is not to deal with sin in His life or a sinful nature, but to model how one ought to live and serve. It becomes a model of living full of the Spirit of God. While there is mystery here, there are also clearly some lessons which we must not miss. Being full of the Spirit is clearly one of the factors that pleases the Father, but what does it mean to be full of the Holy Spirit? What are the aspects of this fullness of God in one's life. In what areas is it expressed? This fullness of God's spirit, which pleases the Father, seems to show up in the five areas in which Jesus had a purpose for His disciples. Jesus' desires for them reflect some of what God has already done in His life. These five areas include: an intimate relationship with God, a close relationship with disciples, godly character, godly thinking, and fruitful ministry.

How does the holiness of the Spirit of God show up in these five areas in Jesus' life? How does Jesus model the standard that He sets for His disciples? Let's look at each one of these and explore the evidence in the passage before us.

✛ CLOSE RELATIONSHIP WITH GOD

In His divinity Jesus is God Himself, so He shares divine nature with the Father and the Spirit. Therefore it sounds a little strange to our ears to ask about Jesus' relationship to God. But in this passage, it is also clear that He is modeling how people ought to relate to God. So looking from the "human point of view," we ask about His relationship with God. **What is implied by the expression "full of the Holy Spirit" (Luke 4:1)? How would this affect Jesus' relationship with the whole Godhead? What other terms or expressions are used to describe Jesus' relationship with the Spirit? What is implied by each about the relationship?**

_____

_____

_____

_____

_____

What do you find in the passage about Jesus cultivating His relationship with God or spending time with God?

_____

_____

_____

_____

One thing implied by the "fullness of the Spirit" is the fullness of God. There are obviously close, intimate relationships that are a result of being indwelt by the presence of God. Being "inhabited" by the presence of God is a metaphor which is not used to describe any other personal relationships. It is this fullness of God's presence, and therefore the working out of His will in Jesus' life, that seems to be one of the things that Jesus is clearly modeling for disciples. To be holy is to live with this kind of intimacy with God and enjoy His full work in and through one's life. It also certainly implies a deliberate developing of one's relationship with Him through communication and fellowship.

✛ CLOSE RELATIONSHIPS WITH A FEW OTHERS

The triune God is a social God. The Being of God is about relationships. To be God in the Christian and biblical sense is to be in relationship. The Father relates to the Son and the Spirit. The Son relates to the Father and Spirit, and the Spirit relates to the Father and Son. All three share in the same holy nature and the attributes of the Godhead, but they exist as three Persons in One and in relationship to each other. Therefore, to be like a holy God is to be a social being. This means being in close relationships with a few other people.

What evidence do you find that Jesus, under the full leading of the Holy Spirit, began to cultivate some close relationships with others?

_____

_____

_____

_____

In choosing the twelve, Jesus has several purposes in mind. He obviously is training leaders for the church and modeling for all how to be a disciple. But He is also doing something more. He is modeling the need for close, human relationships in order to be a holy person like a holy, social God! The classic phrase, "There is no holiness except social holiness," is an expression of this. You cannot reflect the nature of a holy God without reflecting the social nature of God. This means living in close relationships with a few other people who are seeking to follow after God.

This is what Jesus begins to do when He starts calling the twelve around Him. By this means He sets before disciples of all generations the lesson that to be like God, one needs these close intimate ties. Holiness of heart and life demands holiness coming out of godly relationships.

✢ HOLINESS OF CHARACTER

One key expression of holiness is in a person's character. Character is seen in interpersonal relationships. Character shows up when you see how one person relates to another.

There are three major ways in which character is expressed towards others. Two of them we have already observed in the previous section: righteousness and love.

Righteousness is expressed in right conduct, particularly right behavior toward other people. Biblical love can only be expressed in relationships. Love may be expressed in a variety of ways, but it is always towards another person.

The third way a holy character is expressed is in self-giving. This is closely tied with both righteousness and love. Doing the right thing often means the giving of oneself to others. Love also usually means some form of self-giving.

God is a self-giving God. It is part of His holy nature. If His people are to be holy, they have to be willing to give of themselves to other people. Let's see what evidence we can find of these character qualities in Jesus.

▲ Holiness as Righteousness
1. What indicators do you see that Jesus was doing the right thing by walking in obedience to God?

_____

_____

_____

2. Where do you see Jesus saying "no" to evil so that He might say "yes" to God and do the right thing?

_____

_____

3. What evidence do you see that Jesus is committed to a standard of righteousness given by God?

_____

_____

_____

_____

▲ Holiness as Love
What things did Jesus do that lead you to suspect a motive of love or compassion, even where these terms might not appear?

_____

_____

_____

_____

▲ Holiness as Self-giving
1. This category may well produce some significant overlap with the previous two. Self-giving usually comes out of a heart of righteousness and love. Where do you see a self-giving spirit expressed in Jesus?

_____

_____

_____

_____

2. Do you see any examples of a self-protecting spirit in Jesus or one that is looking out for His own interests?

_____

_____

_____

_____

✛ GODLY THINKING

The character of a holy God affects the way Jesus thinks. Because there is a self-giving quality about His nature that is expressed in righteousness and love, He treats people differently. If He were not self-giving, He would be protecting His own interests and He would not be concerned about the interests of others. If He were not righteous, He would not do the right thing or what would be the right or best thing for others. If He did not have a heart of unconditional love, He would not be as concerned about other people and their welfare. So character affects the way we think, especially the way we think about other people.

How does one get the mind of God and think as He thinks? Part of this is related to developing the character of God, but it is also related to getting God's thoughts into our thoughts.

What evidence do you find in this passage that Jesus was trying to communicate the thinking of God to other people?

_____

_____

_____

If you had been present and asked Jesus about the basis of right thinking and of understanding the mind of God, what do you think He would have said to you? What indicators do you find in the text about where He understood the mind of God to be reflected?

_____

_____

_____

_____

✣ FRUITFUL MINISTRY

God is concerned about every disciple's service for Him. He wants everything in its proper order. Before Jesus begins His own ministry, two things are already in place: *His relationship with God,* and *His being (character and thinking).*

The implication of this is that doing (ministry) should come out of relationships and being. Who we are related to and who we are ought to affect what we do for God. What evidence do you find in this passage of a connection between being full of the Spirit and carrying out ministry to others?

_____

_____

_____

_____

Why do you think being full of God would affect what ministry you do and the way you do it?

_____

_____

_____

What forms of public ministry (i.e., to lots of people) do you find in this section? List with references.

_____

_____

_____

_____

What evidence do you find of a private or concentrated ministry to a few?

_____

_____

_____

Jesus has been anointed by the Spirit of God for ministry. God foretold this generations before through the prophet Isaiah (61:1–2). God knows that when His Spirit has control of persons, He can accomplish His will in their lives and in their ministry to other people.

✛ SYNTHESIS

Summarize in five short sentences how the holiness of God through the fullness of the Holy Spirit is expressed in the five major categories in the life of Jesus:

_____

_____

_____

_____

_____

_____

_____

_____

_____

_____

_____

Ask God for insight into how the teaching of Jesus about holiness is matched by a model of a holy life. Then ask the Spirit to make clear whether His holy character is being expressed in your life in these same five ways.

Memory Verses
John 6:69 and Matthew 6:10

Additional Passages for Study

You may wish to study some of these passages more fully during the Word portion of your devotional time.

1. Exodus 19:1–9.
What evidence is there for the five purposes of God in this story?

2. Exodus 20:1–17.
How are commandments two through ten related to the first commandment?

3. Deuteronomy 5–6.
How do commandments two through ten describe the three components of holiness discussed (righteousness, love, and self-giving)?

4. Deuteronomy 7:6–13.
How does this passage reiterate the basic components of God's holiness and our response to each one?

5. Mark 12:28–34.
How does Jesus describe the "First Commandment?" How is this related to the first commandment in Exodus 20:3 and Deuteronomy 5:7?

The Disciples Before and After Pentecost

The goal of discipleship

QUICKENING YOUR THINKING

1. List some good things that you remember about the disciples during their time with Jesus.

_____

_____

_____

2. List some things in your life which you know without a doubt please Jesus.

_____

_____

_____

◆ THE STRUCTURE OF THE BOOK OF MARK
Turn to the Gospel of Mark.

What is Mark's purpose?
Looking at the early chapters, answer the following questions about Mark's Gospel.

1. Does Mark have a genealogy of Jesus?   Y   N
2. Does Mark tell us anything about Jesus' birth?   Y   N
3. Does Mark record the sermon on the mount?   Y   N
4. Checking the closing chapters, how much space does Mark give to the death of Jesus?

A comparison with the other Gospels will show that Mark is the shortest in length and frequently the most brief when it comes to reporting occurrences in the life of our Lord. The history of our Savior is given with machine-gun speed: the stories come in quick succession without much elaboration. Through this straightforward method Mark's purpose appears to be two-fold.

✛ Mark's First Purpose in Writing

Look up the following verses in Mark and indicate how they are similar?
What is the theme which ties them all together?
1:23–24, 27; 2:5–7, 12; 3:11; 4:41; 5:7; 6:2–3; 8:27

_____

_____

_____

These verses all point to Mark's first intention. The identity of the person of Jesus is fundamental to the first half of the book.

Jesus' final examination of the disciples is reflected in the two questions given at Caesarea Philippi in Mark 8:27–28. Some see Jesus as only a prophetic figure, but there is the dawning perceptiveness in the disciples which is reflected in Peter's exclamation, "You are the Christ." The answer of Peter in verse 29 is one crucial point in human history. Emmanuel has come. Jesus is God in the flesh. God, who had revealed Himself to Israel and now to the disciples in the incarnate Christ, can now move to the place of dealing with human sinfulness. This brings us to Mark's second purpose.

✛ Mark's Second Purpose in Writing

Look up these verses and write down the theme that arises the most clearly:
8:31, 34; 9:9, 30–31; 10:32–34

_____

_____

_____

If the first half of the book is taken up with the person of Jesus Christ, the second deals with His death. The book is clearly constructed with a cause (The Person of Jesus: Chapters 1–8) and effect (The Passion of Jesus: Chapters 8–16). Without a clear understanding of **who Jesus is** there is no way to comprehend **what Jesus came to do.** Notice the proximity of the discussion of the cross to Peter's confession. From Mk. 8:30 on, the cross is before Jesus, and none of the disciples fully comprehends the implications of this goal.

Read Mark 8:31–33 carefully.
What is Peter's response to Jesus' talk of the cross?

_____

_____

Having just confessed Jesus to be the Christ (Messiah), why does he so strongly oppose any talk about a cross? What does this say about Peter's conception of the Messiah?

_____

_____

_____

Why do you think Jesus responds so strongly to Peter?

_____

_____

_____

What does it mean to use the name "Satan," and to say, "you are not on the side of God?"

_____

_____

A comparison of various translations will show that the phrase, "you are not on the side of God," can be rendered in different ways. Some say, "You don't think like God thinks." Others have, "you are not minded like God," "you don't have God's viewpoint," or "you are looking at it from a human point of view." You will notice as you read the following chapters that the disciples simply do not comprehend what Jesus is talking about. Let's explore the implications of not thinking like Jesus thinks through an overview of the second half of the gospel.

Our previous look at several verses in this portion of Mark indicated that one of the dominant themes is the coming cross and the death of Jesus. At the same time we also find there is a strong focus on Jesus' time with the twelve. His last months with them before facing the cross in Jerusalem are spent in intensive training of these disciples. So while they have been a part of this ministry in the first half of the gospel, we get even more glimpses of His interaction with them in the second half.

In a broad general way we could say that the first half of the gospel deals with the question, "Who is Jesus?" The second half of the book identifies who the disciples are. The picture we get will give us some indications of the fact that their thinking has not yet been fully conformed to the thinking of Jesus. The resultant story will also give us some insight into how far Jesus has been able to shape their character like His own.

◆ THE CHARACTER AND THE THINKING OF THE DISCIPLES

There are at least five areas of distinct difficulty for the disciples in the second half of Mark.

✥ READ MARK 9:1–13

Look at Mark 9:6 specifically.
What do you think is the possible problem which Peter faced on the Mount of Transfiguration?

_____

_____

_____

▲ _Lack of Spiritual Understanding_

We have seen how Peter, representing the disciples, comprehends only minimally what the Messiahship of Jesus truly means (8:34, Matt. 16:23). But look also at how their comprehension was incomplete on the Mount of Transfiguration. Mark 9:2–6 records that Peter again is speaking with only a glimpse of the glory of Christ. It is understandable that the resurrection would be obscure to them, but 9:10 indicates that they had made no connection with the miraculous ministry of Jesus preceding this chapter and the future of the Messiah.

Note that they actually are debating with Jesus about the demise of the Son of Man in 9:11–13.

It is very clear in all that follows that their spiritual understanding is truncated. They are unable to comprehend the connection between the person and the death of Jesus in any meaningful way. They are still preoccupied with externals. Something must free them to see clearly with spiritual eyes.

✛ READ MARK 9:14–29

What do you think is the deficiency in the disciples at this point?

_____

_____

_____

_____

▲ Lack of Spiritual Power

Note that immediately upon the disciple's descent, they are faced with the problem of a demon-filled boy. Remember that earlier they were appointed with authority over demonic possession (Mark 3:15; 6:13, 30; Matt. 10:8). But here we find them totally unable to meet this basic need which had brought an anxious father to those who were supposed to live with the power of Jesus in offering deliverance from demonic forces (cf. Matt. 16:14–20).

What does Jesus suggest is the way to have the necessary spiritual power?

_____

_____

What is behind this missing element in the disciples? Why are they not empowered for this work?

_____

_____

_____

✛ CONSIDER MARK 9:33–37; 10:35–37

What appears to be the disciples' problem?

_____

_____

_____

_____

▲ Looking After Number One

One thing is quite clear by Mark's use of a recurring contrast. Every time Jesus talks about His self-offering, the disciples are shown as discussing the opposite—how to get what they can for themselves. He is giving, they are grasping (Matt. 20:25–26, Mark 10:35–45). They are focused upon themselves. They vie for position even up through the last journey towards

Jerusalem and Golgotha. The right and left hand of a throne in this culture represents power and prestige, not humility and self-denial. It appears that the competition between the disciples intensifies over the three-year period. The result is that an earlier intense spiritual accountability, which is produced by vulnerability, is lost. We have one indication of that in Judas's growing discontent and outright dishonesty.

✛ Now Look at Mark 10:13–16

What does the contrast between the disciples' attitude towards children and Jesus' attitude toward children tell us?

_____

_____

_____

▲ Lack of Compassion

Why would the disciples refuse a group of children access to Jesus (see Matt. 19:13–15)? Apparently, improper thinking, or not viewing things from God's perspective results in a loss of spiritual vitality, a loss of humility, and a loss of love—even for the weakest and statusless. Note the times in the Gospels where it is recorded that the disciples were the ones who impeded access to the Master for the most needy (Matt. 18:5–6). This is not indicated as a concern for Christ's well-being except when He is visibly exhausted.

Here there is a more fundamental preoccupation with the self which makes every other person a potential irritation to their own attempts at self-importance. Remember that in Luke 9:51–55, both James and John ask Jesus for permission to bring fire out of heaven to burn up a village which was unable to deal with the intensity of Jesus' focus on the cross. Whatever else can be said of these antics, it is readily apparent that the disciples do not possess a true love for many of those around them. In fact, what we see is a consistent misuse of authority and an increasing disdain for the neediest who came to Jesus for ministry.

✛ Read Mark 10:17–24

Why would the disciples be more interested in the rich young ruler than the children of the previous story?

_____

_____

What does this say about their own motivation?

_____

_____

▲ Interest in Wealth, Power, and Influence

The disciples can not be bothered with caring for the children, because the children have nothing to contribute back to them or to Jesus. The children basically require some giving on the part of Jesus and His disciples, and there is nothing to be had in return. By contrast the rich young ruler certainly could contribute something to the apostolic band. He has influence, financial resources, and connections that would seem to be an advantage to the disciples.

Thinking ahead about what would be most advantageous for their own position, the disciples are disappointed that Jesus lets the young man go away. Their concern is not so much for the rich young ruler, as it is for the power he could bring should he join their group. Their motivation, particularly in contrast to their attitude toward the children, is pretty self-centered.

✛ READ MARK 14:32–50 CAREFULLY

What is revealed about the true nature of the disciples in this passage?

_____

_____

_____

▲ Protecting Themselves

The space between the audacious statement of willingness on the part of Peter to stand with Jesus through thick and thin is remarkable next to the verse regarding the level of commitment present at the arrest of Jesus, which reads, "they all forsook Him and fled" (14:50). This painful retreat is heightened by the story of Peter's emphatic denial of Jesus as friend, as master and as the One who loved him in such a unique way (14:66–72).

If it had not been for the women who followed Jesus, there would have been no disciples at the tomb of Jesus, either for finishing the embalming of the body or for the resurrection. This lack of commitment has forced the disciples behind doors of shame, guilt, and self-pity.

Summarize the primary character deficiencies in the disciples.

_____

_____

_____

_____

_____

_____

How would you describe their basic root problem?

_____

_____

_____

_____

▲ Summation of the Character of the Disciples in the Gospels

From this analysis it is not twisting the meaning of the text to say that there is not one good story about the disciples' character between Caesarea Philippi and the tomb of Jesus! It is clear that the heart of the problem of the disciples is their self-centeredness. Peter even believes he has a better idea than Jesus about what the Messiah is supposed to be like (Mark 8:31–32). Peter, like the other apostles, is expecting the Messiah to work by power, and not by sacrifice.

The disciples are so focused upon themselves, they have difficulty understanding what God is saying to them through Elijah and Moses on the Mount of Transfiguration. Their unwillingness to spend time in prayer and dependence upon God limits the spiritual power God can give them for touching lives, like the demonic boy (Mark 9). There is a consistent vigilance about their self-interests when they are discussing who is the greatest and who sits on the right hand and the left (Mark 9:34; 10:37). They are clearly more concerned about themselves than they are others. They do not have time for "little people," like the children who have nothing to give back (Mark 10:13–17). But they are very concerned about wealthy and influential people who might help their cause (Mark 10:17–24). Lastly, they are doing whatever is necessary to protect their own lives, even when that means denying Jesus (Mark 14).

These disciples have clearly come into a personal relationship with Jesus through faith. They have attached themselves to Jesus as disciples for a period of three years. There has obviously been growth and some maturity in all of God's purposes for their lives. But as they come to the end of their time with Jesus, it is obvious that there is a problem with a self-centered focus in their lives that is clearly unlike the self-giving nature of Jesus. While they are out to take care of their own interests, He is concerned about laying down His life for the needs of others. Classic Christian theology has described this problem in terms of a sinful nature or sinfulness. The heart of the problem is self-centeredness.

◆ THE DISCIPLES IN THE BOOK OF ACTS

Most of us in modern Western Christianity are keenly aware of the debates surrounding Pentecost with all of its symbols. While it may not be that everyone will see eye to eye on the need for those externals to be present in a vital spiritual setting, it is undeniable that the internal change in the character of the disciples is what propels the disciples as apostles to storm the known world with what Jesus had transmitted to them. It may be that each of the areas of "lack" has been met by the adequacy of the Spirit of Jesus. Let's take an introductory look at these areas in the disciples' lives. We will return to a more detailed focus on the disciples in Acts in later studies.

✛ SPIRITUAL COMPREHENSION

Take a glance at Peter's first sermon in Acts 2:14ff. As you scan the insights, which include references to the Old Testament and their absolute fulfillment in Christ, coupled with stringent words of judgment regarding Israel's part in the death of Jesus and the present state of their souls, it is not hard to come to the conclusion that Peter has been enabled to see with new spiritual eyes, much like he was able to see only in part at Caesarea Philippi (Matt. 16:17). You remember that Peter had difficulty understanding why the Messiah would not come in power but through self-sacrifice.

What is Peter's view of God's plan for His Son in this sermon (Acts 2:23)?

_____

_____

Peter is clearly beginning to see God has a plan that included the death of His Son and that this was a part of His design from the beginning. It is a radically different understanding of the role of the Messiah than Peter has known before. The difference now is that it is not a comprehension of just one event (Jesus' death) but rather a deep, continual, spiritual perception. Peter and the others think the thoughts of God, but they are also beginning to perceive situations as Jesus would. They are starting to view life and ministry from God's perspective, and this is when their ministry to the world begins.

✢ Spiritual Power

The powerlessness of the disciples at the foot of the Mount of Transfiguration is forgotten as each of the disciples moves into various avenues of expressing their giftedness. The power promised in Acts 1:8 is the life of Jesus given to His own through the ever present ministry of the Holy Spirit. It is always a power like that of the Lord Jesus. It is never once used for manipulation or power control. It is always used humbly, almost self-effacingly.

What examples of spiritual power for ministry do you see in Peter in Acts 9:32–42?

_____

_____

_____

_____

The disciples are now living channels of blessing for every human need, especially spiritual concerns. They are clean vessels through whom Christ continues to minister.

✢ Commitment to Each Other

The nagging internal intrigue of place and power is gone. Those who should be noticed and lifted above the rest, like Peter, are seen as definite leaders but also as encouraging the ministries of others before themselves. Paul's background is forgotten and this former persecutor becomes the head of the church's foreign mission program with much assistance from Barnabas. Even the "pillars" of the early church reflect this when confronted with a volatile issue like the maintenance of the Jewish tradition for Gentile Christians. Rather than an ugly and self-centered debate, there is an understanding of differences within the larger focus on unity, on prayer, on Old Testament truth, and on the Spirit's leading (Acts 15:1–21). As each looks out for the interests of the others, the church is freed from the possibility of debilitating disunity and is enabled to move into every portion of the Roman world without the hindrances of suspicion, distrust, or fractiousness.

✢ Compassion for Others

One thing is clear after Pentecost: it is that these people love in a real way beyond their own personal ability to do so. What evidence do you find of a compassion for the unfortunate in Acts 3?

_____

_____

_____

_____

Every time we read of a contact across racial or national lines, we need to remember the deep-seated prejudice with which intertestamental Judaism had pressed upon these Jewish Christians. Samaria (ch. 8), Caesarea (ch. 10), Antioch (ch. 11), and eventually Rome (ch. 28) are places which carried the stigma of uncleanness for the orthodox Jew. That these disciples not only go, but initiate intimate relationships with Gentiles is a miracle wrought by the sanctifying Spirit of God.

⁜ Bold Identification with Jesus

We tend to quickly forget that the same members of the Sanhedrin, which orchestrated the charges which were to mean the death of the Lord Jesus, are in court when the disciples are brought up for judgment. Against the backdrop of their own betrayal, denial, and rejection, the disciples now stand in radical unswerving boldness (4:13–20). In fact, in Acts there is no account of any reservation in commitment to the Lord on the part of any of the apostles. Nor are they ever shown as being boorish or overly aggressive. Rather in meekness and under the guidance of the Spirit, they move across the known world with unmitigated strength and unbridled purpose. Note the names of Stephen, Philip, Ananias, Peter, Barnabas, and James. No one would question the straightforward approach of the apostle Paul. All of these, and many more, witness to an internal transformation worked by the Holy Spirit. They do not run from persecution, but rather they praise in the midst of it. They cannot help but speak the Name (4:13–20).

⁜ Root of Radical Transformation

Even a superficial comparison of the disciples at the end of the gospel story with their lives in the book of Acts indicates there has been an incredible transformation. They have gone from a lack of spiritual comprehension to significant spiritual discernment. Instead of being without spiritual power for ministry, they are anointed with power. Rather than a rivalry between those within the apostolic band, there is a mutual support and encouragement of one another. Where we previously did not find compassion for people, especially "little people," now we find they are giving time and attention to all who have needs. Whereas before we found them protecting themselves even to the point of denying Jesus, now there is a bold identification with Jesus regardless of the consequences. In the Gospels, disciples often think they have "better ideas" than Jesus, but now their thinking has been conformed more to His way of working.

What root element within the disciples has been changed? How would you describe this transformation?

_____

_____

It is clear that the root problem of self-centeredness has been dealt with in a major way. The disciples' earlier focus upon their own interests and guarding their own positions has now changed. Instead of independent self-wills that are primarily concerned with their own needs, there is a sacrificial giving of themselves that is much more like the character of Jesus. The contrast between the two pictures of disciples is impossible to miss. What has happened is obvious. How this was made possible will be the subject of the next several of our studies together.

▲ Conclusion

It is possible for one who seeks to be a disciple of Jesus Christ to look at externals without connecting those outward actions with a heart of integrity and love. We are called to _do_ something for Him, but our _being_ is in the hands of the Lord first. If He is the Son of Man, then it follows that our life should look like His.

Write here what specific thing the Lord may be bringing to your spiritual attention as you compare your life with the disciples in the Gospels. If you do not sense His leading, then do not

force it. But if there is something in your life that identifies with where they were, would you write that down here?

_____

_____

Is this where you want to be in your own life?

_____

If you would like to know **how** the disciples got where they are as described in Acts, then keep pressing on with these Bible studies. The story will lead us to the way God works if we will continue seeking.

Prayer Suggestion

Is there anything in the lives of the twelve in the Gospels that brings to light something in your life that Jesus wants you to see clearly? If so, ask Him to begin to show you what His solution to this is.

> ### Memory Verses
> Mark 8:34–35

Additional Passages For Study

You may wish to study some of these passages more fully during the Word portion of your devotional time.

1. Matthew 16:1–28.
What additional insights do you find in the disciples' character?

2. Mark 8:22–26.
How does this story provide a picture illustration of the disciples?

3. Matthew 18:21–22.
What does this event reveal about the character of Peter?

4. Matthew 19:16–30.
What does the reaction of the disciples to Jesus' encounter with the rich young ruler reveal about their character?

5. Matthew 26:6–16.
What is revealed about the character of disciples in these two stories?

The Promise of Something More

What was missing after three years of discipleship?

QUICKENING YOUR THINKING

1. Can discipleship fully develop the character of Jesus in believers?

_____

_____

2. After walking with Him as a disciple for some time, are there any areas in your life that are still not reflecting the character of Jesus?

_____

_____

WHERE ARE THE DISCIPLES?

After three years of discipleship training we expect a lot of the twelve. They have had the privilege of being under Jesus' immediate direction of their lives for three years. What do we find when they come to the end of this period? What has discipleship done for a believer in Jesus?

In this study we want to explore some of the results of discipleship. What has Jesus accomplished in the last three years, and what has He not accomplished? Are there some areas that have not been dealt with through the discipleship process? If that is the case, what are these, and how does Jesus intend to deal with them?

Let's approach this subject by asking a question. What is Jesus looking for in His disciples at the end of three years of training? What more does He desire to happen in them to complete His work in their lives?

◆ DISCIPLES WITH SERVANT'S HEARTS
Turn in your Bible to John 12:49–13:38 and read through it carefully.

Jesus is concerned about the life work of His disciples. One of His life objectives has been training them for the ministry He has for them to do. For the past three years He has been teaching them a variety of ways through which they might minister to other people. This training has included preaching, teaching, praying for the sick, casting out demons, discipleship, and personal conversations with individuals. It is a work that centers on touching other lives for God and meeting physical as well as spiritual needs in people.

One of the things Jesus wants to build into disciples is a servant heart, out of which come all these forms of ministry. In this story of Jesus' last Passover, how is He modeling the kind of servanthood that He wants to see in His disciples?

_____

_____

Why is Jesus doing this?

_____

_____

_____

Over Jesus' past three years with the disciples, what are some other ways that He has modeled a servant heart in His relationship with the disciples?

_____

_____

_____

Jesus has been investing His life in disciples in a very costly way. Nothing is more demanding than life-to-life sharing, especially when it is full-time, twenty-four hours a day, seven days a week! Jesus has taken the role of a servant by pouring His life into the disciples and being available to them day and night for the last three years.

This life-to-life investment has several purposes. One of these purposes is to allow Jesus to model a servant spirit. This is why He said, "If I then, your Lord and Teacher, have washed your feet, you also ought to wash one another's feet. I have given you an example, that you also should do as I have done to you. Truly, truly, I say to you, a servant is not greater than his master; nor is He who is sent greater than He who sent Him" (John 13: 13–16).

Jesus is looking for disciples who have servant hearts, i.e., willing to do things a servant would be asked to do, like washing feet. Jesus is not asking them to do something He is unwilling to do Himself. He has come as the model of a self-giving life; on this occasion in the guise of a servant. Servant work is sometimes lowly, often behind the scenes, and frequently without much credit, but Jesus is willing to do it. He wants to see the same heart attitude in the lives of His disciples expressed in service to others.

The disciples have been serving with Jesus in some ways for the past three years. In Hebrew culture the role of students (disciples) with a rabbi entailed some service responsibility. Can you think of some examples where the disciples actually played a servant role with Jesus in ministry?

_____

_____

Who prepared this Passover supper? Check Luke 22:8–13.

_____

Some servant work is being done by the disciples. They observed the servant heart of Jesus, and there is a degree of this in their own lives. However, after the Passover meal the disciples do not

take the servant role and wash one another's feet. Why did they not do this?

_____

_____

Jesus is looking for disciples who have servant hearts. He has modeled this for them in His own life. The disciples have developed a measure of the servant spirit in themselves, but there is clearly a limit to what they are willing to do. They have been trained to do some things in serving God and people, but they are not yet fully like Jesus in this area. Discipleship has made its mark upon their lives, but there is some work still left to be done!

◆ DISCIPLES WITH CLOSE RELATIONSHIPS

We have seen in our studies of the Word that one of God's priorities is relationships. He is concerned about every one of us having an intimate relationship with Jesus and through Him the Father and the Spirit. He is also concerned about disciples developing close relationships with each other. That is part of Jesus' purpose in training disciples collectively. They are trained in a band with other disciples, so that their relationships might develop over a period of years.

It is out of these relationships with Jesus and other disciples that the Lord begins to shape character and thinking, and provide preparation for ministry. The foot washing story means that service from a servant heart ought to come out of our relationships. It ought to be service arising from our relationship first with Jesus and then other disciples.

This relational dimension of our nature is part of being made in the image of God. God is a social being, and when we were made in His image (Gen. 1:26–27), we were all made social creatures. That means that every individual needs some close relationships with other persons.

Jesus, arriving in human form, has the same need. In His divinity, He has close relationships with the other members of the Trinity. But in His humanity, He is modeling for us the crucial need for other close, human ties.

This is one of the reasons Jesus gathers the twelve around Him for the three years of His earthly ministry. To be sure, He is training them to be disciples, but at the same time they are meeting some needs in Jesus' life for close, human companionship. He is committed to twelve out of a larger number of friends and believers. Out of the twelve, He seems to have stronger ties to Peter, James, and John. Many think that out of the three, He is closer to one than the others.

From the story in John 13, with whom does Jesus seem to have the closest, personal tie?

_____

_____

Jesus is not playing favorites. In His supernatural being, He is able to love everyone with the same divine, unconditional love. But humanly speaking He cannot spend the same time with everyone, and therefore chooses to invest His life in a few. This is what discipleship is all about. The disciples are bonded to Jesus, and Jesus is bonded to them.

If Jesus Himself needs close human relationships, what are the implications of this for His disciples?

_____

_____

In this chapter, how does Jesus challenge the disciples to relate to each other "in the same way" He has been relating to them?

_____

_____

Jesus is challenging disciples to love one another as He loved them. What are some of the ways in which He has loved them that He now expects to see in their love for each other?

_____

_____

_____

It would be too strong to say that the disciples do not have any close bonds with each other. They have been living together for three years, and some of them are related by family and friendship ties before they joined Jesus. Do you see any evidence in this chapter of the disciples' friendships with one another?

_____

_____

_____

Are the disciples as committed to one another as Jesus is committed to them? What is the evidence for your answer?

_____

_____

Why do you think the disciples at this stage are not loving as Jesus does and therefore are not fully committed to each other?

_____

_____

_____

The disciples' failure to love one another other as Jesus is loving them is rooted in their self-protection. They are clearly expecting something significant to happen in the near future, and they are still interested in positions of influence in the new "kingdom" that Jesus is bringing. None of them wants to take the lowly place of a servant, much less a slave, and thus be seen as one who is not ready to step into a position of power, influence, and authority. So the heart of their problem is that they are looking after their own interests. This automatically limits their commitment and self-giving to one another!

◆ DISCIPLES WHO THINK LIKE JESUS

Another one of Jesus' purposes for disciples is that they learn to think as God thinks. Part of His task as Rabbi is developing the mind of His disciples, so that they can both gain knowledge and learn a new way of thinking. He wants them to see and ask questions about how God views the world and people.

As Jesus starts His ministry with the disciples, one of His tasks is to give them something to think about. This involves more than knowledge of the revelation of God. It means a whole re-orientation of the mind and the will to see from God's perspective and then act upon it. After three years they clearly understand some things Jesus is trying to teach them, and in some measure He anticipates that they will be able to think in such a way as to reflect His mind and that of the Father.

During Jesus' last evening with the twelve, He continues to shape his disciples. Jesus gives one last teaching, which is recorded in detail in John 14–16. He wants to make sure they do not misunderstand anything. Once more He spends significant time with them in His teaching role.

John 13 is also a record of a significant teaching time. In this story there is a combination of two key ingredients Jesus has been using in order to train disciples. What are the two major ways in which Jesus is communicating truth to the twelve in the upper room?

_____

_____

_____

The disciples have been learning a great deal from Jesus over the past three years. Obviously, their thinking has been shaped by Him in some areas, but not in all. There are certain things about the way Jesus works that they do not yet fully understand. Look again at verses one through eleven. What is the first example in this chapter of disciples failing to understand?

_____

_____

_____

Does Jesus give Peter an explanation on this occasion? How does Jesus explain what He is doing so that Peter can understand?

_____

_____

_____

Look at vv. 18–30. What is the second area where disciples do not understand what Jesus is saying to them?

_____

_____

Look at vv. 36–38. What is the third illustration of something not understood by the disciples?

_____

_____

Why do the disciples not understand these situations? Why have they not formed the mind of Christ after three years under His teaching? Why have they not begun to see the way God works? What is missing in their thinking?

Sometimes the disciples are not thinking as Jesus thought because they lack information. They did not fully understand about the singling out of Judas because they lacked information, specifically about who the betrayer was to be. There are occasions when Jesus needs the disciples to have more information so they can understand what is happening.

However, the real problem here is not a lack of information as much as it is failing to understand the way God works. Peter does not understand why Jesus is washing their feet, because he does not think the way Jesus thinks. He is not thinking about how to serve people. He is thinking as one who wants position and power as well as thinking about how to get them!

Neither does Peter understand why he cannot follow Jesus as he thinks he will. Jesus knows Peter will not follow Him later that evening because Peter will be protecting himself! Jesus understands that in Peter's heart there is significant self-interest and therefore self-protection that will prevent him from fully following. The disciples are not seeing or thinking clearly because of self-interest. There is still a self-orientation about them that does not allow them to think as Jesus thinks, any more than it allowed them to serve as Jesus served.

This story is a good illustration of the way hearts affect heads. A wrong motivation clouds thinking. Failure to have a heart free from self-interest makes it difficult to relate to people as God does, i.e., selflessly. Jesus models for us an unconditional self-giving to others that reflects the heart character of God. This is how He wants to see His disciples living. Yet, they do not yet think this way because they are still thinking about themselves. Their interests are turned in on their own lives, so they do not fully see the way God sees. This means they do not serve people in the same self-giving way that Jesus does.

◆ FULLY OBEDIENT DISCIPLES

One of the things that Jesus has tried to teach the disciples is that their service and ministry to others should come out of godly character. *Who they are* should determine *what they do* for God and for others.

Jesus has also made it clear that one's character is controlled by his will. The choices we make determine what God is able to do to shape our character. When we make the choice to obey God, we reflect His character. The more we obey, the more we look like Him. Character, then, comes out of those choices of our will to be obedient to God. The more obedient we are, the more like Him we become.

When Jesus uses the servant/slave language (verse 16), He raises a picture from the ancient world of master/slave relationships. Since a slave belonged to his master, he was expected to fully conform to his master's will. Whatever the master wanted, the slave did. He was not to be obedient only some of the time, but all of the time. Jesus borrows this figure of speech and gives it spiritual connotations. He looks for disciples that are so absolutely sold out to God that they are like slaves, fully willing to do the whole will of their Master.

In the first part of our reading, how does Jesus Himself reflect being under the full will of the Father?

_____

_____

_____

What other event later this same night will reflect Jesus' own full obedience/total submission to the whole will of God?

_____

_____

So if Jesus is asking His disciples to fully submit to all the will of God, He is not asking them to do something He is not willing to do. His willingness to die for the sins of the whole world is certainly the most difficult thing the Father has asked of anyone. Jesus may be asking us to lay down our lives for Him, but He is not asking us to do anything as difficult as He is asked to do.

What two disciples in this chapter are confronted with being fully obedient to Jesus?

_____

Read again the story in John 13:21–30. Whatever surface motive Judas has for betraying Jesus, what do you think is the underlying issue for him?

_____

_____

_____

Look at the situation with another disciple in vv. 6–9. What is Peter's initial response to Jesus and why?

_____

_____

What is Peter's response when Jesus makes it an issue of His will versus Peter's will?

_____

_____

What is the basic difference between the responses of Peter and Judas?

_____

_____

In the light of vv. 36–38 and what we know happened later this same night, would you say that Peter's submission to the full will of God is complete or not?

_____

_____

How would you explain the fact that Peter is willing to be obedient at some things, but apparently is not totally obedient in every way?

_____

_____

The disciples have learned obedience to Jesus, but it is not a total obedience. The limits apparently come when the cost to one's own person looks very high. Peter certainly is not as ready as he thought he was to lay down his life for Jesus!

Are there any areas in your own life where you find yourself responding like the disciples? Are there any places where you have not been fully obedient to the whole will of God as He has made

it known? Is there any independent self-will that is keeping your will (and therefore your life) from being fully controlled by the whole will of God?

_____

_____

◆ DISCIPLES WHO LOVE UNCONDITIONALLY

Not only is full obedience to the whole will of God an expression of godly character, but love is also an expression of this character. In this story we get a picture of God's self-giving love that keeps on loving no matter what the response.

What references to Jesus' love come at the beginning and end of this chapter?

_____

_____

If Jesus is a supreme example of self-giving love, what expression of that love do you see in this chapter?

_____

_____

In the light of vv. 1–5, what evidence do you see of "unconditional" love in Jesus?

_____

_____

How is this story an expression of Jesus' teaching to the disciples about love in Matthew 5:42–48?

_____

_____

In the story in John 13, are the disciples loving Jesus and/or one another in this unconditional way? What is the evidence for your answer?

_____

_____

Would you say that the disciples loved Jesus in a significant way? How could the closing verses of the chapter be understood to illustrate this (vv. 36–38)?

_____

_____

The disciples seem to have significant love for Jesus, as well as some love for each other, but their love is obviously not yet complete or perfect. They are not loving unconditionally nor are they willing to fully sacrifice themselves for others. Why do you think they are not loving in the same unconditional way as Jesus did?

_____

_____

◆ SUMMARY OF THE PROBLEM

As we have looked at this story of Jesus' time with the disciples on His last night, some interesting things emerge. The disciples have obviously made significant progress in some areas in their walk with the Lord. But it is also clear that there are certain things that are still missing in their lives. In some ways they are like Jesus, but in other ways they are not fully like Him.

✣ LACK OF SERVANT HEARTS

The disciples have been serving with Jesus in a variety of ways, but on this night they are unwilling to serve each other. They have a measure of a servant spirit without a fully committed servant heart. They apparently are looking for the coming of the Messiah with His kingly power, and none of them are willing to take the role of a servant in the eyes of the others. No one wants to take the low position. The heart of the issue seems to be a question of their pride.

✣ NOT FULLY COMMITTED TO EACH OTHER

The disciples certainly have friendships with each other, but it is also clear that there are limits to these relationships. Some close friendships are indicated even in this chapter, yet there is none of the same unreserved commitment that Jesus has to the twelve. They are not loving one another as Jesus loved them, i.e., unconditionally or sacrificially. They have love with some commitment, but it is not the full commitment and intimate relationships that Jesus desires. Again, the problem seems to be guarding one's own position. They are still trying to get ahead and are concerned about their status when the Messiah fully reveals who He is in His kingdom.

✣ STRUGGLING WITH SUBMISSION

The disciples have learned about obedience in their three years with Jesus, but their obedience is not yet absolute submission in every area in their lives. Judas is backing up from his previous commitment to follow Jesus and live in obedience. On the other hand, Peter seems to be moving in the right direction toward a greater surrender. When it comes to head-to-head confrontation, Peter submits to Jesus' will. This certainly is what Jesus desires in all of the disciples. It is also clear Peter's final submission is not finished. The fact that later this night he ends up denying Jesus (John 18:25–27) means there are still certain areas in which he is still willing to protect himself, rather than do the whole will of God! He is committed to much of the will of God, perhaps even most of the will of God. But he is not committed to all of the will of God whatever the cost!

✣ INCOMPLETE LOVE

Lastly, Jesus is looking for disciples to love Him in the same way that He loves the Father and loves them. Jesus wants to see disciples who love unconditionally whether people love them back or not. This is what He has modeled for them in His attitude toward Judas, and this is what He longs to see in their response to Him. But they are not loving unconditionally, even though they love in significant measure. They can even say they are willing to lay down their lives for Him, but in fact this is not really true. There is a measure of love for Jesus, but not the unconditional love Jesus said would fully reflect the heart of the Father (Matt. 5:42–48). The issue still seems to be self-protection rather than full surrender of one's life that allows one to love God with all the heart, mind, soul, and strength.

We have tried to provide an evaluation in these four areas in which Jesus is concerned for disciples. He expects certain things of them, and they do not fully measure up to what He would like to see in their lives. This is not to say that these characteristics are not found at all in their lives, but the full measure of them is not yet true in the twelve.

✥ THE BASIC ISSUE

If you had to describe their basic problem in a succinct way, how would you put it?

_____

Apparently, the disciples are still concerned about their own interests at this point. They have been willing to make some significant commitment to leave certain important things in their lives to follow Jesus. They clearly have been trained as disciples, and that reflects very important choices on their part. But the incompleteness of a servant heart, of their commitment to one another, of their obedience, and of their love for God seems to come out of their own self-centeredness.

These disciples have not fully surrendered their lives to God so He can deal with their self-interest. In theological categories we describe this self-interest as our sinful nature. Some identify this sinful nature as pride and self-will. This seems to fit the picture of the disciples at this stage of their spiritual journey. Other theological terms describing this sin nature are the carnal nature, the carnal mind, carnality, sinful nature, original sin, the old man, and sinfulness. Perhaps our best contemporary description of this problem is self-centeredness. The disciples are still focused on some of their own interests instead of being wholly concerned with the interests of God.

What Jesus gives us on His last night with the disciples is a pictorial description of this significant spiritual problem in their lives. Although they are believers and committed disciples of Him, there is an element of self-focus that has not yet been dealt with in their lives. The real problem in this story in not unwashed feet but unclean hearts. The issue is not dirt but pride! Jesus uses this event as a means of calling to the attention of the disciples (and to us) that even after three years of discipleship, there is a work God needs to do in the heart to deal with pride and self-will. This is the problem.

✥ THE SOLUTION

Jesus does not give us the solution in John 13. But once we have seen the problem graphically illustrated, then along with the disciples, we are in a position to understand the solution as Jesus begins to describe it in chapters 14–16. The law of structure here is problem/solution. The problem is self-centeredness, and the solution is the coming of the Holy Spirit. Jesus introduces the solution in His teaching time with disciples as He tries to prepare them for the coming of the Holy Spirit. In fact, in John 14–16 Jesus spends more time talking about what the Holy Spirit will do in the lives of the disciples than He has taught about the Spirit at any other time with them.

Jesus' leaving has made it appropriate that He should focus on the Spirit's coming. The disciples already know the Spirit in some measure as Jesus makes clear in John 14:17, "You know him, for he dwells with you." But now His discussion of the Spirit's work in disciples' lives is related to the larger issue of the major problem they still face, their self-centeredness.

Jesus has set the stage for the disciples to understand what more they need for Him to do in their lives through His Spirit. This opens the door for us to understand what He means to do for us in our lives as disciples as well. We will explore this solution to the problem for them and for us more fully in the next lessons.

As you go to prayer you may wish to ask God to reveal to you if any of these characteristics of Jesus' disciples (in John 13) are true about your own life. Is there some self-centeredness or self-interest in your life the Spirit needs to uncover so He may help you bring it to Him?

> **Memory Verses**
> John 13:14–16

Passages for Additional Study

You may wish to study some complementary passages during the Word portion of your devotional time.

1. 1 Corinthians 2:6–3:3.
Identify the three types of people Paul describes. What are the characteristics of each?

2. 1 Corinthians 3:3–4:21; chapters 5–6, 8–12.
What evidence do you find of those "of the flesh" (the carnal ones) and what of "the spiritual ones"?

3. 1 Corinthians 13.
How is Paul's word here a solution/answer to the problem of those "of the flesh" described throughout the book? What is the root problem in 1 Corinthians 1–12 that finds its solution in 13:5?

Jesus' Final Preparation of the Disciples

Getting the disciples ready for the Holy Spirit

QUICKENING YOUR THINKING

1. Have you had someone very close to you pass away? How well do you remember your last conversation with them?

_____

_____

2. Jesus' last night with His disciples is recorded in John 13–17. Why do you think John devotes five out of twenty-one chapters in his Gospel to these few hours in the upper room?

_____

_____

_____

THE SETTING

For three years Jesus has been investing His life in disciples. Now He comes to His last evening with them before He goes to the cross, and He knows He will never be with them again in the same way. He will be with them but in a different way. He also knows they are about to face one of the most dramatic experiences of their lives. He is about to leave them and go to the cross, followed by the resurrection. These are going to be difficult days for those who have trusted and followed Him, and Jesus wants to get them ready to face this major trial in their lives.

It should not surprise us that John tells the story of this evening in such detail. Certainly the Spirit of God graphically impressed upon him the importance of recording this evening for future generations of disciples. Since John is most likely "the disciple whom Jesus loved" and this is his last evening with Him, it is natural that he remembers both the events and the teaching vividly and wants to record them for others.

Since Jesus is about to leave the disciples, He takes this occasion to try to help them understand how they are to relate to Himself, the Father, and the Spirit when He is no longer physically present with them. The last three years have been about learning to relate to the Father through Him. Now He is preparing them for relationships with all three Persons in the Godhead when He will no longer be present in the flesh. How He does this is one of the concerns of this study.

The other major concern in this study is to show the relationship between Jesus' teaching and prayer in John 14–17 to the narrative events of John 13. In our previous study we have seen how the story of Jesus washing the disciples' feet in the upper room is illustrative of how far the disciples have come in their training by Jesus and also what they are lacking. While discipleship has made a tremendous difference in God's purposes for their lives, there is still a major problem with their own self-centeredness. This we have seen as a graphic description of the sinful nature of disciples that is expressed in the failure to minister to one another out of a servant heart, and in not loving each other as Jesus desires. It has also been demonstrated by not thinking the way God thinks, not reflecting the character of God by being fully submissive to His whole will, and not being able to demonstrate Jesus' unconditional love.

While the disciples have made progress in all these areas, their self-interest prevents them from being everything Jesus desires. This is the problem described in chapter 13.

We are now ready to see how Jesus addresses this problem in His teaching (John 14–16) and in His prayer for the disciples (John 17). The structure that we are looking at here is that of problem and solution.

◆ KNOWING THE TRIUNE GOD

Turn in your Bible and read carefully John 14:1–15:17. It may be helpful to mark all the references to Jesus (including the pronouns) in red, the references to the Father in green, and those to the Holy Spirit in blue (other colors may be used if these are not readily available).

✧ THE DISCIPLES AND JESUS

God is a personal God and has always made Himself known in person-to-person relationships. He began to do this with Adam and Eve in the Garden of Eden (Gen. 2). Even after sin entered into the world (Gen. 3) and broke the personal relationships, God continued to seek out men and women to know them personally. One example occurs in His relationship with Abraham when He identifies Himself personally and invites Abraham to "walk" before Him and develop the relationship (Gen. 12:1–3; 17:1–8).

The whole Old Testament is a picture of a personal God making Himself known to individuals and then to a nation of people so that all the world might know Him and enjoy the blessings of a personal relationship.

The picture of a personal God gets even clearer with His coming in the incarnation. With Jesus' arrival in the world in the form of a man, God is giving the whole world an object lesson about His own nature: that He is personal, that He relates to people one-on-one, and that He wants every one of us to know Him in a personal way.

Jesus demonstrates this in all His human relationships, and in particular with the twelve disciples. For three years He lives with them so that they spend their days talking, walking, serving, worshipping, and living together. All of this is designed to teach the twelve and all future disciples that they can have a close personal relationship with the eternal God and know Him intimately, just like you can know someone who is your closest friend.

This relationship with Jesus affects disciples in remarkable ways. It affects their relationship with one another. It changes their character to make them like the character of a holy God. It shapes their thinking so that they are thinking more like God than ever before. It also influences their service and ministry for God.

As dramatic as anything else is the fact that their relationship with Jesus now affects the disciples' relationship with God the Father. Jesus puts into their hands certain tools for establishing and maintaining a relationship with God. These are what we frequently call the *means of grace*. They are the spiritual habit patterns that Jesus helps disciples build into their lives, so that they can relate to God. These *means* involve time in the Word of God, time to pray, time to be a part of a small group of other believers following God, and time for public worship. They also include scripture memory, fasting, giving, and the sacrament of the Lord's Supper.

Part of the reason Jesus builds these habit patterns into the lives of His disciples is so they might know how to relate to Him after He is no longer physically present in their midst. The same *means of grace* they use to develop their relationship with God the Father will be the means they will continue to use to relate to Jesus. While He is with them Jesus is helping disciples develop their relationship with the Father. He is getting them ready to maintain their relationship with Him the rest of their lives.

Jesus begins the evening's teaching by trying to quiet the fear of the disciples. It is natural that they would be apprehensive that He is going to leave them. As they face this difficult circumstance, what response is He is asking for from them? Check John 14:1, 11–12.

What does Jesus indicate that He is going to do when He leaves them and why?

⁑ The Disciples and the Father

After Jesus begins to prepare disciples for His own leaving, He talks about both His relationship to the Father and that of the disciples with the Father. What does Jesus say about His own relationship with the Father (vv. 5–11)?

Jesus is giving us some significant insight into the nature of the Trinity. He is indicating that there is a oneness in the essence of the being of God, whether this essence is expressed as Father or as Son. This oneness of being is reflected in Their oneness of will, oneness of mind, and oneness of character. This oneness is sometimes described as the three Persons of the Trinity interpenetrating each other. The technical word is "coinherence," meaning all three Persons of the Godhead share this same essence of being and therefore all the attributes of the Godhead. What are the implications of this? Perhaps they are best seen by asking the question, "What does a relationship with Jesus mean to us as we seek to know the Father?"

What does this mean about the disciples' current relationship with the Father?

What does Jesus say about the future relationship of disciples both to Himself and the Father in vv. 18–24?

_____

_____

_____

Jesus is talking about an indwelling of the Godhead in His disciples. He speaks about disciples being in Himself and He in them. Up to this point in their lives they have known Jesus as one person knows another. But because He has been in human form, they have only known Him externally as teacher and friend. Now He is talking about a much more internal experiencing of Himself and the Father, where there will be an "inhabitation" of the disciples by Himself and the Father. If knowing Him as teacher and friend has provided some sense of intimacy with God, He now begins to talk about an even greater intimacy where the Father and Son can dwell within disciples.

Jesus introduces another relationship right before (14:16–17) and right after (14:25–26) this discussion of the indwelling of the Father and the Son (14:18–24). What is it?

_____

_____

_____

The context indicates that Jesus' discussion about Himself and the Father indwelling in disciples is closely wrapped up with His discussion of the coming of the Holy Spirit. Jesus speaks more this last evening about the coming and the work of the Spirit than He ever has before. We must observe carefully the context in which He does this. He is talking about the Spirit's work in relationship to the work of the Father and the Son. It is the interweaving of these themes about all three Persons of the Trinity (John 14–16) that have made this section of Scripture so central to the church's understanding of the Triune God.

✛ The Disciples and the Spirit

In preparing disciples for His own leaving and their future relationship with Himself and with the Father, Jesus now begins to talk about the role of the Holy Spirit (John 14:15–17, 26). What are the various names that are given to describe the Spirit?

_____

_____

What is the relationship of the world (i.e., non-believers) to the Holy Spirit?

_____

_____

What is the current relationship of the disciples to the Holy Spirit?

_____

_____

The disciples already have a relationship with the Holy Spirit. Jesus has just responded to the disciples' question about how they could know God the Father. Suppose they had asked the question about to how they might know the Holy Spirit. How do you think Jesus would have answered them?

_____

_____

In light of what Jesus has already said, it would seem obvious that His response to the disciples would be the same as His response to Philip (v. 9). The principle is, if you have seen one member of the Trinity, you have seen all three. Since Jesus is the one they have seen and known best, to see and know Jesus is to see and know the Father and the Spirit.

The implications of this are that if disciples want to know something about the attributes or the character of the Triune God, they only have to look at the attributes and character of Jesus. To see one is to see all three. To know one, i.e., to have a personal working relationship with one member of the Trinity, is to have it with all three.

The disciples have learned about the whole Godhead from seeing Jesus. God is about relationships, character, thinking, and ministry to others. Having learned this by knowing Jesus, they now understand that God the Father and God the Spirit are about these same things as well.

Jesus has indicated that they already know the Holy Spirit because He already dwells with them. What is He indicating will be different about their relationship to the Spirit in the future?

_____

_____

How is this related to the future relationship of disciples to Jesus and the Father (vv. 20–23)?

_____

_____

It may be a temptation to say that at this point the disciples are only related to Jesus in an objective way, i.e., He is outside of themselves in His own physical body, and therefore, this is the way they are related to God. At the same time Jesus is now suggesting that in the future there will be an indwelling of God in their hearts.

There certainly is going to be a subjective change in the future, but it may be too strong to say that disciples are only related to God objectively at this point in their lives. Clearly, God has been working in their lives through His Spirit to change their character, motivation, and heart. When they repented of sin and began to believe in Jesus, something happened internally in them. They have experienced the new birth, which means there is an inner transformation that is wrought by the Holy Spirit (John 3). It would not be accurate to say there has been no work of God subjectively within disciples.

At the same time, Jesus makes it clear that there is going to be a fuller "inhabitation" of disciples by all three Persons of the Trinity in the near future. In the plan of the way God works, this is related to God's unfolding purposes throughout history. People have related to God the Father throughout the Old Testament in a personal way. With the coming of Jesus in the Gospels they are learning to relate to Him more fully, person to person. Now with the coming of the Holy Spirit they will relate still more fully in terms of knowing God in all three Persons. This is not to suggest a rigid dispensationalism that limits the Old Testament to God the Father, the Gospels to Jesus, and the rest of the New Testament to the Holy Spirit. Rather, there is a flow of God's unveiling Himself so that people might know Him as a Triune

God more fully. This process will be completed when the Spirit comes at Pentecost.

It is perhaps best to understand the unfolding of God's purposes in relationship to the three members of the Trinity as something other than a timeline that might imply one stage of knowing God as being left behind and moving on to something else. A picture of concentric circles in probably a better way to view this unfolding revelation from God. The inner circle would be God's revelation of Himself in the Old Testament, the next circle would be God speaking through His Son in the Gospels, and the third circle would be God's unfolding of Himself through the Holy Spirit in the rest of the New Testament.

Unfolding Revelation of the Godhead

It is the work of the Spirit coming at Pentecost that will then be the full indwelling of the personal presence of the Triune God in disciples. They have already known Him, just like they have known the Father and the Son. At Pentecost they will know Him in a more intimate way than they have ever known before. With the coming of the fullness of the Holy Spirit, they will know the fullness of the Father and the Son. Knowing one and enjoying an intimate relationship with one, will be the same as knowing all three and enjoying an intimate relationship with all three.

The first thing the Spirit will do when He comes at Pentecost will be to come with the Father and the Son so that disciples have a fuller experience of the Triune God and a deeper intimacy with Him. God will be known subjectively in the inner experience and lives of disciples in a greater way than has ever been possible before.

If the coming of the Spirit on the day of Pentecost provides a clue to the full possibility of knowing the Triune God, there is something else that is closely related to the coming of the Spirit as well. It has to do with the work of the Spirit in solving the problem we have seen described in John 13. The relationship between the disciples and Jesus up to this point has been good, but clouded at times with self-centered hearts. Their sinful nature, i.e., their self-centeredness, has meant that they have followed Jesus with divided hearts. At times they wish to do what Jesus did and so submit and obey Him. At other times they have their own interests at heart and want to go their own way instead of Jesus' way.

The promise of the coming of the Spirit is related to providing disciples with an undivided heart. Jesus is looking for disciples whose will is wholly one with His will, with the Father's will, and with the Spirit's will. When He begins to pray for them, He is seeking this oneness with His disciples like the oneness He has with the Father. This will mean a oneness of intimacy, a oneness of character, a oneness of will, a oneness of purpose, and a oneness that comes out of a self-giving heart instead of a self-protecting heart.

After Jesus describes the coming of the Spirit as the context for understanding the future relationships between disciples, the Father and Himself, He turns again to the discussion of the disciples' on-going relationship with Himself. John 15:1–17 is about how disciples are to *abide* in Jesus. Here Jesus uses the great analogy of the vine and the branches to describe this future tie between Himself and disciples. It is a figure of speech (metaphor) that describes how disciples are to draw life from Jesus and continue to maintain their relationship with Him.

What does Jesus indicate is to be the natural result of this abiding in Him?

_____

_____

What are the two results that Jesus indicates are to come from bearing much fruit?

_____

_____

How does this abiding in Jesus relate to the context of the coming of the Holy Spirit?

_____

_____

Jesus is expecting disciples to obey His commandments, abide in His love, and love one another as He loved them, i.e., unconditionally and sacrificially. How is this related to the larger context of the coming of the Holy Spirit?

_____

_____

_____

Sometimes we treat the first part of John 15 in isolation from its larger context. We must understand it in the light of Jesus' Trinitarian discussion and particularly in the light of the coming of the Holy Spirit. Disciples have already had a relationship with Jesus, so continuing this is one thing. Continuing with the intimacy of a vine to a branch and with the power to fully obey in love is now going to be closely related to the work of the Spirit in their lives. The Spirit's coming not only provides an internal work of God in the lives of disciples, it also is a reference to the fullness of God through His Spirit that enables disciples to draw upon the life of Jesus, fully obey all that He asks, and love sacrificially as He has loved them.

Jesus is continually commanding the disciples to love one another with the agape love with which He has loved them (John 15:12, 17; 13:34–35). Is He commanding them to do something and not providing a way for them to do it? The context suggests that in fact He is expecting the Spirit to do a work in their lives that will enable them to do just what He is asking them to do.

With this possibility in mind, let us turn our attention to the coming of the Spirit as a solution to the problem we have seen in John 13. You will remember part of this problem is the inability of the disciples to fully submit/obey and their inability to fully love as Jesus loved. There are other dimensions of the problem, so let us look at how the coming of the Spirit affects disciples within this whole evening's context.

◆ THE COMING OF THE HOLY SPIRIT
THE SOLUTION TO THE PROBLEM: PART 1

The coming of the Spirit, first of all, provides the opportunity for a more intimate relationship with the Triune God. His first task is to provide a deeper relationship with God the Father, God the Son, and God the Spirit. This is what our story has been about so far. The Spirit's second task is to address the problem of self-will we saw illustrated in John 13.

In addressing this problem of self-will in disciples, there are *two parts of the solution*. In part one, *the Holy Spirit comes to act as the agent of the solution*. As described in John 14–16, the coming of the Spirit means that the solution to this problem is the personal, ongoing presence of the Triune God through the Holy Spirit. God Himself will deal with the problem through His personal presence fully dwelling in the lives of individuals.

This will involve the surrender of one's will and therefore one's life to the full indwelling presence of the holy God. The surrender of the will (and therefore the self-centeredness) is what makes it possible for God to assume full control so that His will is worked out in the will of a disciple.

Part two of the solution involves Jesus' prayer for the sanctification of disciples (John 17:17). *Sanctification is the content of the solution itself.* It involves God's actual transformation in the lives of individuals. He began to do this when they started following Jesus (initial sanctification), and has continued to do it throughout the three years of their discipleship training (progressive sanctification).

His prayer for their sanctification in John 17 is for a full sanctification, whereby the twelve are to be made more completely like Jesus, holy as He is holy. This is what *sanctification* is all about: it means *to make holy*. When the full presence of the holy God dwells in people through the Holy Spirit, the result is that a disciple is made like the holy character of God. It is this holiness of character that is the solution to the basic issue of self-centeredness.

The problem of self-will is dealt with when the will now fully reflects the will of the Holy One. This is the place to which Jesus wants disciples to come, so they will no longer reflect part of His will and part of their own will. Rather, because God has all of them, they will be fully reflecting His life, character, thinking, and ministry to the world.

This work of the fullness of the Spirit and full sanctification is expressed in four ways. You will recognize these four things as parts of the problem described in John 13. They involve the issues of ministry to others, relationships with others, thinking, and character. The overall structure of this section of John makes it clear that we are dealing with a problem/solution pattern. John 13 has clearly identified the basic problem of self-will manifesting itself in a lack of servant ministry, in less than fully bonded relationships, in thinking that does not reflect the mind of God, and in character that it is neither fully submissive nor fully loving.

When we come to look at God's solution in John 14–17, we find all of these areas addressed. The overarching structure of problem/solution (John 13–17) means the discussion of the coming of the Spirit will address the problem, sometimes implicitly and sometimes explicitly. The fact that the Spirit's coming is laid out so fully after the problem is so graphically described, makes it clear that the Spirit is the One who is going to address this problem in the lives of disciples.

In addition, the specifics of what the Spirit does are also described. This means there is also an explicit description of how the Spirit provides an answer to the problem of self-will. Let's look at some of these explicit parts of the solution that God is going to provide when His Spirit comes fully in disciples.

✛ EMPOWERING FOR MINISTRY

The whole passage suggests that Jesus' discussion of the coming of the Spirit means that the Spirit is going to deal with the self-centeredness of disciples that has kept them from serving one another in their ministry with Jesus. Only when there is a surrender of their wills to the will of the Spirit, can the Spirit then help them reflect the ministry of Jesus to other people. This is the implicit part of the solution to the problem of self-centeredness and ministry.

As you look at John 15:26–16:11 what are the explicit areas in which the Spirit's coming will assist disciples in ministry?

_____

_____

_____

✣ Relationships with Other Disciples

The problem we have seen in John 13 is that the disciples are not closely committed to one another because they are too busy looking out for their own self-interests. Jesus' challenge to them is that they are to love each other "as He loves them," i.e., be bonded and committed to one another in the same way He is to their lives. When Jesus discusses the coming of the Spirit, He implies that when His Spirit comes, He will empower disciples to relate to one another in the same way Jesus relates to them. This is another part of the implicit solution to the problem that has been described.

To explore the explicit part of the solution, let's look at the section John 15:12–17. What is the key command that Jesus gives to disciples about their relationship with each other?

_____

_____

_____

How many times is this repeated? Why the repetition?

_____

_____

What is the contrast between this attitude the disciples are to have with one another and the attitude they may expect to have from the world toward them (15:18–27)?

_____

_____

_____

What is implied about the way the Spirit (vv. 25, 26) is to assist them in facing both challenges?

_____

_____

_____

The third problem area for the disciples is not thinking as God thinks. Their perspective on people and themselves is not God's. God needs to reorient their thinking by taking out their self-centered approach to life.

In John 14–16, the Spirit of God seems to be clearly committed to right thinking. How many times in this section is the Holy Spirit described as the "Spirit of truth"?

_____

_____

What does this tell us about the Holy Spirit?

_____

_____

From John 14:25–26; 16:12–15 what does Jesus teach the twelve about the Spirit's effect on their thinking?

_____

_____

_____

_____

_____

_____

The Spirit speaks for the Father and the Son. If He is part of the Triune Godhead, this should not surprise us. When one of them speaks, they all speak! The Spirit is concerned with communicating God's truth to disciples, helping them recall what God has already taught them through Jesus, and preparing their thinking in such a way that they approach people, the world, and life from God's perspective.

✛ CHARACTER

The fourth problem area for the disciples in John 13 is that of character. Theirs is a character that is not submissive nor fully obedient to God and a character that does not love as God loves. Both of these dimensions are part of the problem. In being disobedient and not fully loving, the disciples are not reflecting the character of Jesus nor the character of a holy God in righteousness and love.

In looking for clues to see how the Spirit of God is going to work the character of God into disciples, we begin with His name. What is the adjective that is attached to the Spirit of God that is our normal way to refer to the Spirit?

_____

_____

The Spirit of God is referred to more than ninety times in the New Testament with this adjective. Why do you suppose God's Spirit is not described by some other adjective, emphasizing His love, mercy, righteousness, etc.?

_____

_____

Jesus said that the Father would send the Holy Spirit "in My name" (John 14:26). What is the implication of the name/nature of Jesus in relationship to the Spirit?

_____

_____

What adjective describes the Father in John 17:11?

_____

The overall picture is that a Holy God, who has manifested His holiness in the character of Jesus, is now going to send His Holy Spirit to do a further work in the lives of disciples. Part of this work will clearly have to do with their character, since this holiness reflects the character of God.

Look in John 14:15–15:17. What references do you find here to the two dimensions of God's holy character that were lacking in John 13?

_____

_____

Apparently, a disciple must be willing to make some character choices so the Spirit then can empower the disciple to reflect the holiness of God in love and obedience/righteousness. Jesus said, "If you love Me, you will keep My commandments. And I will pray to the Father, and He will give you another Counselor" (14:15–16). It is the choice to love God fully and be fully obedient to Him that is a part of the full submission and consecration of one's life to receive the Spirit of Jesus in this full way.

When a disciple chooses to love and keep walking in obedience, this means he can experience not only the fullness of the Spirit but the fullness of the Father and Son as well (14:20–24).

The discussion of these exhortations to love and walk in obedience is implicitly tied up with the whole discussion of the coming of the Spirit. Jesus clearly means for His disciples to understand that His challenge for them to love and obey in this way is not without His desire to assist them. He has wanted them to walk in love and obedience before. Now He discusses these character traits in the context of the coming of the Spirit. The obvious implication is that the Spirit is going to empower them to do this in a way that they have not been able to do up to this time in their lives. If they _choose_ to love and obey fully, Jesus is sending His Spirit to _enable_ them to fully love and obey.

✦ SUMMARY

It is clear then that the discussion of the coming of the Holy Spirit is set in a context of the larger teaching of Jesus to disciples about their relationship to Himself and the Father, on the one hand, and about the needs in their own lives, on the other. The coming of the Spirit is not in a vacuum. He comes to address certain needs. One is the need for deeper intimacy with the Father and Son as well as with the Spirit Himself. Another is the need described so graphically in John 13 that focuses upon the disciples' self-centered nature. The Spirit desires to come, not only to provide intimacy with the whole Triune God, but to purify disciples of independent self-will and provide a heart that is like the heart of a holy God. This heart then will express itself in an empowered, self-giving ministry to other people, relationships of unconditional love with other disciples, thinking that is reflective of the mind of the Triune God, and a character that expresses the holy character of God in righteousness/obedience and love. It is the Spirit of God, who comes as the agent of a holy God, to make all this a reality.

Prayer Suggestion

Ask the Spirit to show you any area of your life that He, with the Father and the Son, has not fully inhabited. Pray in the Spirit about your ministry to others, your relationships, your thinking, and your character to see if there is anything God the Father and God the Son have not fully taken over in your life through God the Holy Spirit.

> ### Memory Verses
> John 14:16–17

Additional Passages for Study

You may wish to study some of these passages more fully during the Word portion of your devotional time.

1. John 14.
Make a detailed outline of the entire chapter.

2. John 14.
What are the major responses from a disciple that Jesus is looking for?

3. John 15:1–17.
Make a list of everything said about how disciples are to relate to Jesus.

4. John 15:18–16:11.
List all the relationships of a disciple to the world.

5. John 16:16–33.
List everything Jesus is saying to His disciples.

Jesus Prays for Disciples

The role of full sanctification

QUICKENING YOUR THINKING

1. When you listen to someone praying, does this give you any hints about their relationship to God and/or about what is really important to them? Why?

_____

_____

_____

_____

2. If this is true, what would listening to Jesus' praying to the Father tell us about Their relationship and about what is on Jesus' heart? Answer from your memory of His prayer in John 17.

_____

_____

_____

_____

◆ TEACHING AND PRAYING: JOHN 14–17.

Turn in your Bible to John 17:1–26 and read through it prayerfully.

✣ HOW JESUS PRAYS

We have been focusing our attention on Jesus' teaching of disciples during His last evening with them. In preparing them for His own leaving and their future relationship with Himself, with the Father and with the Spirit, He has been giving them specific instructions recorded in John 14–16. The new part of this instruction has been His intense teaching about the coming of the Holy Spirit. When Jesus comes to pray in John 17, does He pray about the coming of the Holy Spirit?

_____

_____

_____

What do you think is the central petition of Jesus for His disciples?

_____

_____

_____

_____

While Jesus mentions several things in His prayer, the focus of His intercession seems to be for their sanctification (17:17). To be sanctified means to be made holy (i.e., "holified"). God is described as the Holy Father (17:11) and the Spirit of God has been described in Jesus' teaching as the Holy Spirit (John 14:26). If the Spirit of God is to be the agent of the Triune God in the life of disciples, is it possible that Jesus' prayer for making the disciples holy (i.e., for their sanctification) is really a prayer for the coming of the Holy Spirit in a fuller way in their lives?

It may be that on this occasion Jesus is using two different ways to talk about the same thing. What we have in this section (John 14–17) are (a) His promises that speak of a fuller work in the lives of disciples that is to be accomplished by the Spirit, and (b) His prayer for their sanctification that has to do with the actual activity of transformation that the Spirit is going to work in the individual. For some within the Body of Christ, this is why the experience of full sanctification (described in John 17) has been equated with the coming of the fullness of the Holy Spirit (described in John 14–16).

Most agree that the fulfillment of Jesus' teaching about the coming of the Holy Spirit comes on the day of Pentecost in Acts 2. It also would seem natural to see the experience in Acts 2 as the fulfillment of Jesus' prayer for the sanctification of disciples. If the day of Pentecost is not the answer to Jesus' prayer, then we do not have one. How unusual it would be if the Son of God, who is holy, prays to the Holy Father to make disciples more holy, and there be no answer to His prayer! The logical implication of the flow of the materials is that, in fact, the prayer for the sanctification of disciples, as well as the fulfillment of the teaching about the Holy Spirit, both find their fulfillment on the day of Pentecost.

✛ THE SEQUENCE OF JESUS' LAST EVENING WITH DISCIPLES

Looking at the overview of the way God has worked on this last evening of Jesus with His disciples, this is what we are seeing. The sequence of events seems to be the following:

1. _John 13_ describes _the problem_: The disciples are still very self-centered even after three years with Jesus. They do not have full servant hearts, they are not fully bonded to each other, they are not thinking as God thinks, and they are not reflecting the character of Jesus in submission/obedience or love.

2. _John 14–16_ gives _the solution (the agent)_: The Holy Father is going to send the Holy Spirit in the name of Jesus to His disciples. This will involve the indwelling presence of the Triune God through the Holy Spirit and a solution to the character problem the disciples have at this point. This must involve a surrender of self-will to the full will of God so that the Spirit of God can work out God's will in the lives of the disciples.

3. _John 17_ is a request for _the solution (the activity)_: The Holy Son prays to the Holy Father to make the disciples holy (i.e., to sanctify them). It is the full sanctification of the disciples that will deal with their self-will and give them the character of a holy God.

4. *Acts 2 is the fulfillment* of the teaching about the Holy Spirit and *the answer* to Jesus' prayer for the sanctification of disciples: The Holy Spirit fills the disciples at the day of Pentecost and sanctifies them in response to Jesus' petition.

◆ SANCTIFICATION OF DISCIPLES: SOLUTION TO THE PROBLEM: THE ACTIVITY OF GOD

After Jesus finishes His teaching of disciples, He begins to pray. When a person starts praying, it is possible to learn some things that reflect their heart as well as their head. Jesus' prayer gives us some insight into the priorities in His own life and His burden for the disciples. He still desires something more for them from the Father.

In the first part of Jesus' prayer, He shares some things that indicate what He has already done by way of modeling for the disciples (17:1–10). Then in the second part of the prayer He begins His petitions that indicate what He still desires God to do for them (17:11–26).

✢ JESUS' MODEL

As Jesus prays, He gives to the disciples and to us a picture of what He has been doing with His own life and what He has been trying to set before the disciples as priorities for them. It will be difficult to escape the conclusion that these are exactly the same priorities we have seen in His desires for disciples in John 13 and in what He expects the Holy Spirit to do for them in His teaching in John 14–16. These areas include the following:

1. Intimacy with God

Jesus is modeling the kind of intimacy He wants to see every disciple have with God. One of the indicators of this in His prayer is the description of Jesus' relationship with God as that of a Son to a Father (v. 1). It is the intimacy of a family relationship, and it becomes the dominant picture of the relationship between the first and second Persons of the Trinity throughout the rest of the New Testament. This is reinforced by the fact that Jesus is praying and communicating with the Father. There is a closeness suggested by the fact that He prays, as well as by the way He prays.

What other evidence of this intimacy between Jesus and the Father do you see in the chapter?

_____

_____

_____

The sense of closeness is certainly indicated by the petition of Jesus to the Father to glorify Him in the Father's own presence as well as a reference to living in the permanent presence of God before the creation of the universe (v. 5). A further indication of this intimacy comes in the frequent references of Jesus to being one with the Father (vv. 11, 22–23). Finally, the repeated mention of the Father's unconditional agape love for the Son reinforces the picture of intimacy between these two (v. 23–24, 26).

2. Fruitful Ministry

Jesus indicates that He has glorified the Father by doing the ministry that God asked Him to do. "I glorified Thee on the earth, having accomplished the work which Thou gavest Me to do" (v. 4). The entire Gospel story expands our understanding of what this work is that Jesus has done. However, in the immediate context of this evening in the upper room it has an obvious reference to His work of discipling the twelve. He will also fulfill a work of the Father on the cross the next afternoon, but that work has not already been accomplished; it is still to come. The reference here has to do primarily with Jesus' life work before His death.

What are some examples mentioned in this chapter of the work of discipleship Jesus has already accomplished in the lives of the twelve?

_____

_____

_____

_____

The first work Jesus has accomplished in the lives of the disciples is to give them eternal life (John 17:3). This life is explicitly described in terms of knowing the Father and knowing Jesus. "This is eternal life, that they know Thee, the only true God, and Jesus Christ whom thou has sent" (John 17:3). Eternal life is obviously tied to a personal working relationship with Jesus and His Father. Jesus has certainly made this possible for the twelve.

It is also clear that Jesus has by means of life-to-life sharing made known (manifested) the essential nature (name) of God (John 17:6). By reflecting the holy nature of the Father, Jesus has revealed to them what godliness is supposed to be like.

Further, Jesus has made known to them the Word of the Father (John 17:6, 8, 14); to have a personal relationship with God is to communicate with Him verbally. This means receiving His words as an expression of His person. No personal relationship can develop without communication, so the Word Jesus brings is clearly a vehicle that makes it possible for disciples to know the Father better and better.

Thirdly, Jesus has been praying for His disciples (John 17:9). We see an example of this in His prayer for them in this context. However, this is probably suggestive of the fact that He has been talking to the Father on their behalf for the past three years.

While Jesus has been accomplishing these things directly in the lives of the disciples (modeling the nature of God, giving them the Word of God, and praying to the Father for them), He has also been modeling for them the importance of this work as the heart of making disciples. The result is that He has been giving them a tool they will use when they in turn go to make other disciples for Him.

3. Close Personal Relationships
What evidence do you see in this chapter of the work of Jesus in creating close relationships between disciples?

_____

_____

_____

_____

Jesus is illustrating the crucial importance of this close bonding in His own relationship with the twelve. The very context that they are in, i.e., the upper room for the Passover and a time for teaching and prayer, is illustrative of the kind of close intimacy Jesus wants to see in the future between the disciples. Not only this, but together they have received Jesus' ministry in their lives and have responded to Him and to the Father.

4. *Godly Thinking*
Jesus has just spent a part of the evening sharing certain teaching from the Father with the disciples (v. 1) in order to help shape their thinking. What else do you find in the context of vv. 6–11 that is suggestive of what Jesus has already done to influence their thinking?

_____

_____

_____

The consistent giving of the Word of God to the disciples is obviously a major factor in Jesus' attempt to shape their thinking. His evaluation is, "I have given them the word which thou gavest me" (John 17:8, 14). So they are hearing truth from the Father. Their response has been to receive the Word of God and to keep it (17:6, 8). Certainly this is suggestive that their minds, as well as their wills, have been influenced by understanding what God is saying so that they can respond affirmatively to whatever He says to them.

5. *Godly Character*
Jesus indicates that He has manifested (i.e., revealed) the name of the Father (v. 6). Since *name* in the ancient Near East referred to nature or character, the revelation of the name of God is a revelation of the character of God. Jesus has been demonstrating this very name/character to the disciples in Himself. What is the key adjective that describes this nature of the Father in vv. 1–11?

_____

What other components of the holy nature of God are revealed in this chapter?

_____

_____

_____

There are eleven references in this chapter to things God "gives." This may well be indicative of the grace (self-giving) of the Father. He is also described as the righteous Father (17:25) and the Father who loves unconditionally (17:23, 26). If the reference to Jesus' sharing with the disciples the Word is also connected with the truth of God's holy character, truth would also be an expression of His nature (17:17).

✜ SUMMARY

Make a list of the five things that Jesus has modeled for disciples as a part of accomplishing God's work on earth.

_____

_____

_____

_____

We notice that Jesus has set before the disciples something of 1) the intimacy He desires to see them have with God, 2) the ministry He longs to see coming from their lives, 3) the relationships He wants them to have with one another, 4) the thinking He would like to see in their minds, and 5) the character that reflects the character of a holy God. What the disciples still lack in these areas (cf. John 13) is what Jesus indicates the Spirit is going to provide in their lives (John 14–16). Now, in His prayer Jesus reminds them that He Himself has been modeling all of these things for the past three years. He is not asking them to commit themselves to anything that is not a part of His own life and ministry.

✣ Jesus' Petitions

▲ "Keep them in thy name"

The first petition (v. 11) is for the Holy Father to keep the disciples in His own name or character. This is the same name/character which the Father has given to Jesus. It is the giving of that holy character to the disciples that will make it possible for them to experience being "one" in the same way that Jesus is one with the Father, i.e., one in holy character.

Jesus has guarded the disciples in this new nature that He has already been imparting to their lives (v. 12). Throughout the discipleship process He has kept them walking with God and growing in this new nature. Only Judas has been lost of the original group. Now Jesus is coming to the Father, and He begins to pray for a protection and for a keeping of the disciples when He is no longer physically with them.

Why do the disciples need protection? What does Jesus say about the relationship between the disciples and the world in vv. 14–16?

_____

_____

_____

_____

This petition of Jesus for the Holy Father to keep the disciples in His name/character is a reference to earlier stages of sanctification. God begins to make disciples holy, i.e., shape their nature/character when they start following Him (sometimes called *initial sanctification*). It is the discipleship process with Jesus that has protected them from the evil one as they have grown in godly character (sometimes called *progressive sanctification*). In initial sanctification and in the growth of progressive sanctification, i.e., the progressive developing of His holy name/character in their own lives, they have been guarded from the evil one. This leads then to the next petition that Jesus has for His disciples regarding a fuller work of sanctification.

▲ "Sanctify them"

The second petition is for the Father to sanctify (i.e., make holy) the disciples in a way that they have not yet been made holy. Since they already know something of the Holy Father's nature in their own character and they have lived in the presence of Jesus and have been protected in this shared name/character for the last three years, Jesus' petition now for them has to do with an additional work of God in their lives. In fact, this petition to sanctify disciples is the heart of Jesus' prayer.

If the Father answers this prayer and sanctifies the disciples, what will they look like? What will that affect in their lives? The passage gives us some significant hints, and not surprisingly, they fall into the same categories we have been discussing regarding the needs of the disciples.

1. *Greater Intimacy with God*
Where in vv. 17–26 do you see evidence of this greater intimacy?

_____

_____

_____

_____

     This deeper intimacy as a result of full sanctification is suggested by Jesus' petition "that they may all be one, even as thou, Father, art in me, and I in Thee, that they also may be in us" (v. 21). This oneness that He desires to see in the disciples, first of all, reflects a kind of intimacy that the members of the Trinity have with each other. Jesus then elaborates, "I in them and Thou in Me that they may become perfectly one" (v. 23). Jesus reinforces this with His promise about "I in them" (v. 26) as a part of this fuller work of God in their lives. He desires to continue this intimacy with them into eternity, so He makes it clear that it is His desire that the disciples be with Him and behold the glory that He has known before the foundation of the world (v. 24). Therefore, being made more holy is related to knowing Jesus more fully in this world as well as in eternity.

2. *Fruitful Ministry*
The petition to sanctify disciples is related to Jesus' desire for them to be involved in ministry to others. What evidence do you find for this in vv. 17–26?

_____

_____

_____

_____

     Apparently this fuller work of sanctification will empower the disciples to go into the world in the same way Jesus was empowered to go into the world (v. 18). It will make a difference in their ability to do the work of God in the same way Jesus did it. That should make it possible for them to glorify God on the earth, and when they finish their lives, to be able to say they have "accomplished the work which He gave them to do" (v. 4).

3. *Close Relationships with Other Disciples*
     Jesus is praying for the disciples to experience sanctification together. The more like a holy God they become, the more like one another they become. This is part of the bonding process in the development of their own personal relationships.

     In addition, Jesus' desire for the disciples to be one in the same way that He and the Father are one is a part of the unconditional, loving commitment He wants to see between disciples (vv. 21–23). Further, the love that the Father has for the Son is what Jesus wants to see in the disciples for one another and this love is to come as a result of what Jesus is going to do through their sanctification (v. 26).

4. Godly Thinking

What are the immediate contextual indicators (vv. 17–26) that sanctification is related to godly thinking?

_____

_____

There may be a great number of ideas about what sanctification/holiness is all about. Jesus is praying that the disciples will be sanctified according to the truth of what a holy life is to be like as revealed in the Word of God. Since God's Word is the source of truth, the Word will be the pattern of what holiness looks like. The biblical standard for holiness of heart and life was certainly different from that of Israel's neighbors. Jesus is making it clear that the content of a sanctified (i.e., holy) life will have to be defined by God, not by someone else.

Jesus' prayer also implies that sanctification will assist the disciples in understanding the truth of God's Word, and therefore, this experience will make them more effective in sharing the Word with others.

5. Godly Character

The nature of sanctification is to make holy. Therefore, the petition to sanctify the disciples is a petition to make them more holy than they already are. This is consistent with the nature of a holy God, who is already beginning to give His holy name/character to the disciples. Now Jesus prays that the Holy Father will do something further to make the disciples more like a holy God.

Two aspects of this holiness of character are revealed in a further description of the Holy Father in vv. 25, 26. What are the two character traits of God mentioned in these verses?

_____

_____

We have seen that Jesus has been looking for a fuller obedience from the disciples earlier. It is obedience that leads to right living and therefore to an expression of righteousness in life. He has also been looking for a greater love than they have known before, and now He talks about making more fully known to them the love He has experienced from the Father.

Two major expressions of the holiness of God's character come in terms of righteousness and love in relationships with other people. Jesus apparently wants to see these two things worked out in His disciples, and He desires to meet needs in their lives so that this will be possible.

✣ REVIEW OF THE EVENING

The whole evening of Jesus with the disciples fits together. It begins with a narrative story of the disciples' failure and self-centeredness (John 13). In this story we get a picture of the major problem the disciples are facing, namely, their self-centeredness.

This is followed by the teaching of Jesus in chapters 14–16 with a special accent on the coming of the Holy Spirit. The Spirit seems to be bringing the full Trinity into the lives of the disciples in a way they have not known before. He also is coming bringing the solution to the problem that is pictured in John 13.

After describing the coming of the Spirit, Jesus begins to pray for the sanctification of the disciples. This is His way of praying about the effects of the coming of the Holy Spirit in the disciples. His petition for the disciples matches the areas of need they have (John 13) as well as His description of what the Spirit of God is going to do when He comes (John 14–16). All of this strongly reinforces the conviction that we have a clearly laid out sequence:

1. A statement of the problem.
2. A statement of the agent of the solution.
3. A petition for a full solution to the problem.

The implication of this sequence of materials is that the need of disciples to have God do something about their self-centered, sinful nature is related to the coming of the Holy Spirit. The full coming of the Spirit in the lives of the disciples on the day of Pentecost is intimately tied up in Jesus' desire for full sanctification of the disciples. It is this kind of evidence that leads to the equation of the fullness of the Spirit with full sanctification. One phrase describes the agent of God's activity (Holy Spirit) and the other the actual work of God in the life itself (sanctification). They are two complementary ways of describing what God desires to do in disciples.

Prayer Suggestion

Pray through the prayer of Jesus, making the petitions for yourself instead of for someone else.

> **Memory Verses**
> John 17:17–18

Additional Passages for Study

You may wish to study some of these passages more fully during the Word portion of your devotional time.

1. John 17.
Make a detailed outline of the entire chapter.

2. John 17.
Make a list of everything Jesus wants to see happen that has not yet happened.

3. John 18:1–27.
What happens in this story that further illustrates the basic problem of the disciples described earlier in John 13?

4. **If the problem of the disciples in John 13 (and 18) is self-centeredness and self-protection, how does Jesus model the opposite in John 18:28–19:22?**

When the Holy Spirit Comes

What happens when you are filled with the Holy Spirit?

QUICKENING YOUR THINKING: ACTS 1:1–11

1. What is Jesus' final command to His disciples? His last promise?

_____

_____

_____

2. What is the significance of the fact that these are the last things He says?

_____

_____

_____

GETTING PERSPECTIVE
Turn in your Bible to Acts 2:1–13 and read through it carefully.

✧ SYMBOL AND REALITY

In any discussion of the coming of the Holy Spirit, there is always an immediate interest in the symbols of His coming. Make a list of the symbols you see in this passage.

_____

_____

In addition to the symbols, there is some symbolic language that is very important. These "symbolic terms," like symbols, point to something else. What symbolic words do you find in this passage?

_____

_____

God is a master teacher. When He wants to communicate something, He usually states it in words and then often gives us a symbol as a complementary description. Symbols are things that point to the reality that God is trying to communicate. For example, the symbol of the tabernacle in the Old Testament points to God's personal presence dwelling among His people. Many other symbols represent God, like a cloud, thunder, fire, a whirlwind, a personal conversation, angels, written words, etc. All of these are valuable, and some are used more often than others. The point is that the symbols are not the presence of God themselves; they represent the presence of God. The reality is God Himself; the symbols only help people understand and experience the reality of God.

It is very important to make this distinction regarding the event of God coming in His fullness on the day of Pentecost. He gives us certain symbols and symbolic terms. All of them are valuable, but they only point to the reality of God's personal presence with His people. *Great care must be taken to not spend so much time on the symbol that the reality is missed.*

✣ THE CONTEXT IS ESSENTIAL FOR UNDERSTANDING THE COMING OF THE SPIRIT

In the light of our previous studies it is particularly important to be aware of the context of the coming of the Spirit. This is something that Jesus has both promised and prayed for. You will remember that He began to set the stage for this by clarifying for the disciples two major problems which they had in John 13. One problem was the fact that He was leaving them, so that they would no longer be living in His immediate presence. The other problem was their self-centeredness, illustrated in their unwillingness to assume the role of servant. There will be no understanding how the Holy Spirit relates to a solution to these problems without recalling the problems themselves.

When we come to Acts 1–2, we are dealing with the solution to the twofold problem described in John 13. The coming of the Spirit is an experience which must be understood as the fulfillment of Jesus' promise of a solution in John 14–16 and as an answer to His prayer for a solution in John 17. In other words, on Jesus' last night He sets the stage for what is to come by providing a picture of the problem as well as His solution. In this way He is getting them ready for what He desires to do on the day of Pentecost. Any attempt to isolate the events in Acts 1–2 from this larger context is full of incredible dangers.

✣ THE WAY GOD WORKS: HISTORICALLY AND PERSONALLY

Many times in scripture there are unique historical events described, and at the same time there are individuals who personally experience something with God in the midst of that historical event. It is important to understand that two things are happening at the same time. Historical events, of course, are unique and unrepeatable in regard to their immediate setting and their place in time. However, the fact that people are experiencing something with God in the midst of these events is often a pattern that God desires to set for future generations.

An example of this combination of historical events and personal experience is Jesus' call of the disciples to follow Him and become "fishers of men" (Matt 4:17–21). When Jesus first calls them by the Sea of Galilee, it is a definite historical event in which He is inviting them to be the first group of disciples. This is not repeated in the future in exactly the same setting, not even with the other disciples He calls or with other generations of disciples. Future disciples will not be called by the Sea of Galilee while they are working with their boats and nets.

At the same time, Peter, Andrew, James, and John are individuals who are experiencing a call from Jesus. It is this personal experience of being called to follow Jesus that He *does* want repeated to potential future disciples, so they can follow Him in the same way. While others will not be called in the midst of identical physical and geographical circumstances, they will be called to the underlying principle to follow and be personally related to Jesus. This *is* a repeatable experience, and Jesus desires it for all future disciples. So in one sense, Jesus' call to the disciples in Matthew 4:19 is a unique, unrepeatable experience. In another sense, it is a personal experience for believers that Jesus desires to happen repeatedly in the lives of future individuals.

This perspective is important in understanding what is happening on the day of Pentecost. There is a unique historical event that is happening here, and we do not want to miss the significance of this. The symbolic word "Pentecost" stands for the second of Israel's major festivals. Each of the Hebrew festivals symbolizes a historical event in the life of Israel. The Passover symbolizes their Exodus from Egypt. The Feast of Tabernacles symbolizes their wandering in the wilderness. The Feast of Pentecost symbolizes the giving of the law at Mount Sinai. It is that occasion which is understood to be the birth of the nation of Israel.

Thus when the Holy Spirit comes "on the day of Pentecost," that special day raises immediate connotations for the Jewish participants. It symbolizes the birth of a new Israel of God and the coming of the presence of God in a new way, parallel to the coming down of God at Mount Sinai to meet Moses and the people of Israel (Exod. 19–24).

This means that what happens at Pentecost is in one sense a unique, unrepeatable historical experience. It is the birth of the early church, and that only happens once. At the same time, the 120 believers and disciples of Jesus experience a work of the Holy Spirit in their lives in a personal way. God does intend this work to be repeated in the lives of future believers, just as much as He intends others to learn to "follow Jesus."

The emphasis of our study here will be on the personal experience of the disciples which is repeatable in the lives of future believers. We are presupposing that Pentecost should be understood as a historical event and the birth of the early church. The birth of the church is an obvious result of the coming of the Holy Spirit and is an unrepeatable experience.

However, our focus is going to be on the personal experience of the 120 in the upper room when the Spirit comes: *It is not only possible to repeat what happened to them, but it is desirable.* We will concentrate our attention on the effects of the coming of the Spirit in their lives and try to discern the underlining principles which indicate which effects ought to appear when the Holy Spirit comes in His fullness in the lives of other believers in future generations, including our own.

⁘ THE FULLNESS OF THE SPIRIT IS FOR BELIEVING DISCIPLES

Those whom Jesus challenges to wait for the coming of the fullness of the Spirit are those who had been with Him for the past three years. They exercise repentance and faith when they first come to know Jesus (Mark 1:14–15). Then they make the additional commitment to trust Him and become His disciples (Mark 1:16–20). They become fully convinced that He is the Messiah and confess their faith in Him in that role (Mark 8:29; Matthew 16:16). Further, their faith in Him continues to increase as they walk with Him and know Him better (e.g., John 2:11).

So the experience of the coming of the fullness of the Holy Spirit is definitely not an initial experience of God's saving grace. It is something God has for believing followers of Himself, particularly those who have been His serious disciples.

◆ THE INFILLING OF THE SPIRIT OF THE FATHER AND OF THE SON

Focus in your Bible on Acts 2:1–13 and mark every key word which you think is significant in this section.

⁘ THE PROBLEM OF INTIMACY WITH GOD

Jesus has been trying to get the disciples ready for His leaving. But it still comes as a shock when they realize they will probably never see Jesus again in the same way as they have up to this time. The departure of Jesus' physical presence raises the question of future intimacy with Him. Will the disciples be able to know Jesus and the Father in the same in-depth way they have for the past three years?

Jesus tells them not only that the same kind of closeness they have known with Him will be available, but that there now will also be a greater intimacy possible. How does Jesus describe this deeper relationship in John 17:22–23?

_____

_____

_____

_____

In Acts 2:4 the Holy Spirit comes upon disciples. What is the verb used to describe His coming?

_____

How does this word imply a greater intimacy than disciples have known before?

_____

_____

Jesus has described His previous close relationship with His disciples by using a friendship metaphor. "You are my friends if you do what I command you. No longer do I call you servants, for a servant does not know what his master is doing; I have called you friends, for all that I have heard from my Father I have made known to you" (John 14:15). Friendship implies a great deal of intimacy, yet Jesus now is talking about a "filling" of disciples with the presence of the Spirit and therefore the presence of the Father and Son. This seems to be related to His promise that both Father and Son would indwell disciples and make Their home with them (John 14:20, 23).

Does "inhabitation" imply a greater degree of intimacy than friendship?

_____

_____

If disciples are filled with the Holy Spirit, then they will know the fullness of the Father and the Son. What do you think are the implications of being full of the Spirit of God and therefore full of the Triune God?

_____

_____

_____

It is difficult to miss the Trinitarian nature of what is happening in Acts 1-2 (1:2–8; 2:27, 32–33). The implication of all of this Trinitarian data is that the coming of the fullness of one member of the Trinity, i.e., the Holy Spirit, means the coming of the full presence of the whole Triune Godhead. Therefore, when the Spirit fills the disciples, they are also filled with the presence of Jesus and the Father. To be filled with the Spirit is to be filled with God. To know the fullness of the Spirit is to know the fullness of God's presence, direction, and will in one's life.

✛ The Symbols of God's Full Presence

We have already discussed the role of symbols that point to a reality God wants His people to experience. What two symbols seem to represent the presence of God in Acts 2:1–4? Why do you think these symbolize the presence of God?

_____

_____

_____

_____

The *tongues of fire* seem to be one of the symbols which represent God's presence. It rests upon each of them as a slice of flame, so that people can see the full presence of God resting upon them. Fire is used often in the Old Testament as a symbol of God's presence. It comes in the burning bush when God meets Moses on Mt. Sinai (Exod. 3). It also appears in thunder and lightning when God comes down on the mountain to meet Israel after the Exodus (Exod. 19). We see it again in Elijah's contest with the prophets of Baal on Mt. Carmel (1 Kings 18).

It is appropriate that it appears here. Those present at Pentecost know the Old Testament, and they would not miss the symbolism that this fire points to the living God. Fire, of course, is not the key thing; the key thing is God's presence. The symbol points to the reality. The symbol of fire, signaling God's full presence in the lives of believers, does not occur again in the New Testament. But the reality of God's full presence certainly does appear (e.g., Acts 8).

Wind is the second of the symbols which seems to be particularly appropriate for identifying the Spirit of God. The Hebrew word for spirit is *ruah*. It symbolizes "wind," "breath," and "spirit." The Jews understood that when you talked about the breath of God or the wind of God, you were talking about the Spirit of God. In Greek, the word *pneuma*, also means "wind" and "spirit." In both Hebrew and Greek there is a close identification of wind with spirit, making wind a particularly apt physical symbol of the Spirit of God.

Wind was something which you could not see, so it is described here in terms of the sound of the wind, which makes one aware of its presence. This is a particularly appropriate symbol of the presence of God because it represents a very powerful force at work, and yet one which you cannot see. Wind does not appear as a symbol of the full presence of the Holy Spirit elsewhere in the New Testament, but again, the reality of God's full presence does appear at other times.

✛ Summarizing: The Answer to the Problem of Intimacy

How would you summarize God's answer in Acts 2 to the problem of intimacy?

_____

_____

_____

_____

The first problem of a close, intimate relationship with God seems to be addressed on the day of Pentecost by the full presence of God coming through His Spirit. By filling the disciples, God is indicating the fullness of His presence in their lives. He desires for them to know Him in the fullest way possible and for them to be under His full direction and control in every part of their lives.

The question raised here is whether God's full presence can come and take complete responsibility for the life of a person unless that person voluntarily surrenders his will and life to God. If a person continues to maintain control over his own life, how can God's Spirit be fully in charge? This question raises the second problem which the disciples have: their own self-centeredness. This problem is addressed with a different description of the coming of the Spirit, and this now becomes the focus of our attention.

◆ THE BAPTISM OF THE HOLY SPIRIT
Turn in your Bible to Acts 1:1–11 and read carefully.

✥ THE PROBLEM OF SELF-WILL

The second problem that the disciples face is the issue of their own self-centeredness. They are so busy looking after their own interests that they can not selflessly give of themselves in a servant ministry to one another or to Jesus. They are not loving as Jesus loved, they are not thinking as Jesus thought, nor are they fully submissive to God's will for their lives. The root of this self-interest seems to be their independent self-will.

The disciples started surrendering their wills to Jesus when they became believers. Then as they walked as disciples, they continued to give Him more and more of their lives, but it is obvious from Jesus' last evening with them that they are still working primarily out of a concern for themselves. They are not fully submitted to the whole will of God in every area of their lives.

The solution needed is a radical dealing with self-centeredness. The answer to the problem of independent self-will is a transformation of this self-centeredness. This is frequently described in scripture in terms of cleansing or purification. It does not mean the destruction of the will; the will is a central part of our human personhood. Our will is one of the things which distinguishes us from other parts of creation. We will never lose our volitional capacity to make choices. But is our will controlled by our own self-interest, or is it surrendered to God to be controlled by His will? The crux of the matter is the whole issue of surrender of the will and the resulting cleansing of our self-orientation.

✥ HOLY SPIRIT—THE AGENT OF CLEANSING

After raising the problem of the disciples' self-centeredness in John 13, Jesus then begins to promise the coming of the Holy Spirit in John 14–16. The implication is that the agent to deal with this problem is God Himself coming through His Spirit.

In Acts 1:5, how does the term "baptism" relate to the question of "cleansing" or "purifying" of a life? To put it another way, what does the physical symbol of baptism with water suggest?

_____

_____

In Hebrew culture, to baptize with water implies a washing or a cleansing from something. The term "to baptize" seems to be used in several ways in the New Testament. Jesus uses it to refer to the baptism of John with water (Acts 1:5). What do you think is being symbolized by this baptism of water for those who are turning to God?

_____

_____

How could being "baptized with the Holy Spirit" (1:5) be understood differently from being baptized with water?

_____

_____

If being baptized with water implies the washing away of sins and guilt, then the baptism of the Spirit may well be symbolizing a washing away of self-centeredness. It may be the term used for the purifying of life from one's independent self-will, so the will can become wholly God's.

✤ ONENESS OF WILL THROUGH SANCTIFICATION

Jesus' prayer for the full sanctification of the disciples may have to do with this internal surrender to the will of God. When He asks that they may be one even as He and the Father are "one" ("I in them and thou in me, that they may become perfectly one" John 17:23), He is talking about a oneness of the will which leads to oneness of character.

The question is whether the disciples have completely surrendered their will to the full will of God. Has that full surrender of the will led to a purification of their lives from the self-centered orientation that comes from an independent will?

Read carefully through Acts 1:15–26.
In this story, what evidence do you find that the disciples are moving away from seeking their own will and asking God for His will?

_____

_____

_____

_____

✤ SYMBOLS OF DEALING WITH SELF-WILL

Baptism is obviously a symbolic term that implies a washing away of something unclean and undesirable. This means the "baptism of the Holy Spirit" implies a washing away of something, and it seems to be best understood in the context as a cleansing from self-centeredness.

Do any of the other symbols on the day of Pentecost relate to this idea of purification or cleansing?

_____

_____

We have already discussed how fire is a symbol of the presence of God in the Old Testament. It is a particularly appropriate symbol, because when God comes under the symbol of fire, He comes for one of two purposes. He comes for judgment, so fire symbolizes that something can be consumed or destroyed. But He also comes to purify, and so fire may also imply a purification, as in the case of the "refiner's fire" (Mal. 3:2). In summary, when the fiery presence of God comes, it comes either to judge people for sin or to purify people from sin.

In this case, the fire symbolizing God's full presence would seem to imply a purification of the lives of the disciples. It is purifying in the sense of burning up self-centeredness, so the life is purely centered on God. Again, this does not imply the destruction of the will, but purifying it from self-interest.

✢ RELATIONSHIP OF THE BAPTISM TO THE INFILLING OF THE HOLY SPIRIT

If there are two problems being presented on Jesus' last night with the disciples, then it should not surprise us that two parts of the solution are proposed in Acts 1–2. When we look at the purposes of God's solution in these two areas, we begin to see how complementary God's work is in the lives of the disciples.

How do you think the two terms for the coming of the Holy Spirit, (a) the baptism of the Spirit and (b) the infilling of the Spirit, represent God's answer to the two problems which the disciples have?

_____

_____

_____

How do these two parts of God's answer complement each other?

_____

_____

_____

The problem of a close, intimate relationship with God seems to be addressed on the day of Pentecost by the full presence of God coming through His Spirit. By filling the disciples, God is indicating the fullness of His presence in their lives. He desires for them to know Him in the fullest way possible and for them to be under His full direction and control in every part of their lives.

The problem of self-centeredness is addressed by cleansing the disciples from their self-orientation through the baptism of the Spirit. God deals with the disciples' independent self-will by washing away their self-centeredness (baptism of the Spirit). Only when there is a radical dealing with the sense of independence can God come in His full presence through His Holy Spirit to take possession of an individual (infilling of the Spirit).

God's presence is related to the will. Where a disciple's will is still partially controlled by himself, God does not have full control and His presence cannot be fully expressed. But where the will of a disciple is fully surrendered, then God, through His Spirit, can come to take total control of the will and therefore the life. Now choices of the will can be made in harmony with God's will. The Spirit is able to make known God's will (without the interference of an independent spirit) and enable the disciple to keep on choosing God's will.

The implication of this is that the cleansing of self-centeredness in the disciple (answer to problem two) makes it possible for the full presence of God to come through His Spirit (answer to problem one). This means that purity and presence are two sides to the same coin. Until a life that is controlled by the will, has been surrendered and purified of self-interest, God's full presence can not dwell there. When this has been done, God can come and fill the individual, so that He fully controls them by His immediate presence.

Therefore, the first results of the coming of the Holy Spirit have to do with the full presence of the Spirit of God indwelling an individual and the purifying/cleansing of the self-will so that one can enjoy the full measure of His presence. These two things occur simultaneously, even though we have separated them for the purposes of analysis. When this happens, there are some other results which follow. However, it is important to note that the other effects of the coming of the Holy Spirit happen because of these two primary things. When independent self-will has been cleansed and the whole presence of the Spirit of God comes, it is expressed in four major ways. We will look at each of these in our next study. But before we do that, we need to examine what disciples have to do so the Spirit can come.

◆ THE CONDITIONS FOR THE COMING OF THE HOLY SPIRIT

Jesus is leaving and the time is short. His last instructions are for the disciples to wait! He has something more for them and does not want them to depart from Jerusalem until they receive the promise of the Father (Acts 1:3–4).

But how are they to wait? What is going to make them receptive to this promise from Jesus? What do they do during this waiting time in order to receive the fullness of the Spirit? The question is particularly relevant to us because, as disciples of another generation, we need to know what the conditions are for us to receive the fullness of the Spirit.

While the story is in narrative form, we find in Acts 1 the conditions for the coming of the Spirit in His fullness upon the disciples. We will have to draw them out from the narrative rather than finding them in a list; nevertheless, they are there.

▲ Presuppositions

We have already referred to the fact that the disciples and others in the upper room are clearly believers in Jesus. They have repented and believed, they have started walking in faith, and they all have a personal relationship with Him. The disciples, in particular, symbolize this close relationship of committed followers of Jesus. Thus in any discussion of the coming of the Holy Spirit, we are presupposing that this is for believing Christians.

We are also presupposing that Jesus' last evening with the disciples made it obvious to them that they had at least two significant problems. One was the problem of how to closely relate to Jesus once He left them physically, and the other was the problem of their self-centeredness. By the time the disciples have gone through their upper room experience plus the arrest, trial, crucifixion, and resurrection of Jesus, there is no doubt in their minds that they have some areas of serious need in their own lives. Jesus has promised to meet these needs (John 14–16), and this certainly stands behind their responses to Him in this chapter.

Having presupposed, then, that those seeking the fullness of the Spirit are 1) committed believers 2) who realize their need for God to do something more in their lives, what are the other specific conditions for receiving the Spirit that seem to be indicated in this chapter?

There are *three important conditions* that are illustrated in this story. The first is a *definite seeking* of the Spirit as the fulfillment of what Jesus has promised. The second is a *total consecration* of their lives to God. The third is a *total trust* in Jesus to send His Spirit fully into their lives. Let's look for the evidence in each of these areas.

✛ A DEFINITE SEEKING OF THE SPIRIT AS THE PROMISE OF THE FATHER
Focus your attention on Acts 1:1–14.

1. What evidence do you see of the disciples seeking the Holy Spirit?

_____

_____

_____

_____

2. How serious were they in their seeking? Perhaps an indication of this may be the amount of time the disciples spent in the upper room. Pentecost came fifty days after the Passover. Jesus was crucified on the Passover and rose three days later. Does that give us any indication how long the disciples waited for the coming of the Spirit?

———————————————————————————————————————

———————————————————————————————————————

3. What is implied by this kind of serious seeking of the Holy Spirit?

———————————————————————————————————————

———————————————————————————————————————

———————————————————————————————————————

If persons wait upon God for a day, you know they are serious, but when they wait upon Him for a week, you know they are deadly serious! In this case we have not one person seeking God in this way, but one hundred and twenty. Certainly they are reinforcing each other's desire to hear from God and receive the promise of Jesus. This kind of seriousness definitely implies a hope to receive the promise from Jesus. They had learned to trust Jesus, so they expect Him to fulfill His word regarding the promise of the Father.

Waiting this long may also suggest some significant recognition of their own need. They have been given an assignment to go and make disciples of all nations, so they have a large lifetime ministry assignment ahead of them (Matt. 28:19). Yet, after their last night with Jesus, it is clear that there is something not right in their relationships with Jesus and something else is wrong within themselves. Their recognition of these needs may be a motivation behind their serious seeking of the Lord.

It is very possible that the disciples remember Jesus' earlier instructions to them about how one receives the Holy Spirit from the Father. Check Luke 11:9–13. What does Jesus say is the way one receives the Spirit?

———————————————————————————————————————

———————————————————————————————————————

It is possible that the two other conditions for receiving the Spirit may also be implied by their giving of this kind of time and energy to get an answer from God. One of those conditions is a total consecration of themselves to God and the other is a total trust. Let's look for further evidence of these two things.

✢ TOTAL CONSECRATION OF THEMSELVES TO GOD

On Jesus' last evening with them, He says to them, "If you love me, you will keep my commandments, and I will pray to the Father, and He will give you another Counselor to be with you, even the Spirit of truth" (John 14:15–16).

1. What evidence do you find that the disciples are choosing to love Jesus at a deeper level and are willing to fully obey Him? Focus your search in Acts 1:1–14.

———————————————————————————————————————

———————————————————————————————————————

———————————————————————————————————————

The words "love" and "obedience" do not appear in this chapter, but we have evidence in pictorial form that the disciples are moving toward a deeper commitment to Jesus. They apparently are loving Him enough to be willing to fully obey. Their return to wait in Jerusalem and their willingness to wait at least a week are good indications of their new serious desire to be fully obedient to God's will for their lives.

2. What evidence do you find that the disciples are moving toward a fully surrendered will to the whole will of God?

_____

_____

_____

_____

You will remember that there was a time when the disciples could only look out for their own individual positions and statuses. They were pushing themselves forward, sometimes to sit on the right hand and on the left of Jesus, other times wanting to know who among them was the greatest. Pride and self-seeking have been quite characteristic of them in the past.

By this time in the story, however, there seems to be a different attitude in their hearts. For example, we see in the choosing of the twelfth apostle a perfect occasion for rivalry and self-seeking to be expressed. Instead, two men are put forward, and by consensus the disciples agree to seek the mind of the Lord. They are asking God to make known His will regarding this choice. "Lord, who knowest the hearts of all men, show which one of these two thou hast chosen" (1:24). This may well be an indicator of the disciples' move towards the full surrender of their wills to the whole will of God. Each disciple would have certainly had some preferences as to whether Joseph or Matthias should have been selected. But instead of pushing forward "their candidate" or their wishes, they are seeking God's mind about His will. This is a strong indicator that they are moving toward full consecration of their wills to the full will of God.

3. How does this kind of full consecration begin to address the problem the disciples have faced of their own independent self wills? In other words, how is consecration a solution to the problem of self-centeredness?

_____

_____

_____

_____

If the heart of the disciples' character problem is a focus upon themselves and their own personal interests, then the only way to deal with this problem is a giving up of their "rights" to God. It is this giving up that is the process of total consecration to the whole will of God. This means that the will is no longer self-centered or independent of God's direction, but is fully surrendered to the whole will of God. There can be no full consecration without dealing with the question of the independent self-will. As we see disciples moving to a place of letting God have His way instead of pushing "their way," we begin to discern that they are getting close to the place where their own independent self-wills are being given over fully to God.

✦ A Total Trust in Jesus to Do as He Promised

From the beginning of the disciples' relationship to Him, Jesus has asked them to put their faith in Him (Mark 1:15). They have been through different levels of faith as they have learned to trust Him more fully over the last three years. Now the question is whether or not they can trust Him in an even greater way.

1. Many times biblical narratives give indicators of "faith" or "trust" in God without mentioning the word. What implicit evidence do you see in Acts 1 of the disciples moving toward a deeper level of trust in God?

_____

_____

_____

_____

One indicator of the disciples' trust in Jesus is their obedience to His command to return to Jerusalem and wait for the promise of the Father. This obedience implies a tremendous trust in Jesus to send His Spirit as He had promised. They have learned to trust Jesus over the past three years, so they have a great confidence that He will do as He has said. A further indication of this full trust in Jesus is expressed in their determination to wait as long as necessary for Him to fulfill His promise. They trust Him enough to wait a week, seeking the Spirit that He has told them will come.

The disciples' faith in the Lord is also related to their surrendering to God the choice of a twelfth apostle. They are coming to the place where they can trust Him to make the choice, rather than having to insist on their own best judgement. The surrender of their right to make the choice is an indication of the fact they have a greater confidence in God's ability to choose for them than in their own capacity to have things their own way.

2. How is this total trust related to the issue of total consecration? To ask the question in another way, why would they be willing to consecrate themselves fully to God's will for their lives?

_____

_____

_____

_____

Jesus is looking for disciples who are moving to a new level in their relationships with Him, the Father, and the Spirit. He has asked for both commitment and faith before; now He is looking for these at another level. He wants the disciples to deal with their problem of self-will by coming to the place of total consecration to Him. He is looking for a surrender of their will so that they might have the whole will of God. In order to do this, they must trust God with everything they are surrendering to Him. Total trust is the reverse side of total consecration. If we are not willing to totally trust someone, then we will not totally commit ourselves to that person. Jesus is looking for both, wrapped in the same decision.

Summarize in your own words the three key conditions for the coming of the Holy Spirit.

_____

_____

_____

_____

As you come to the end of this study, you may well be aware that Jesus is not only looking for these three conditions in His own disciples, but He is looking for them in us as well. The question is, are we ready to fully trust Him?

Prayer Suggestion

Thank God for the availability of His cleansing power to take away our self-centeredness and to give us the fullness of His presence. You may also be ready to pray about the coming of the Spirit in your own life through a definite consecration of yourself to Him and a total trust of your life into His hands. If you are ready for all that God has for you, do not hesitate to seek Him for this.

> **Memory Verses**
> Acts 1:4–5

Additional Passages for Study

You may wish to study some of these passages more fully during the Word portion of your devotional time.

1. Acts 1.
Make a detailed outline of everything leading up to Pentecost.

2. Acts 1.
Identify every significant person described in this chapter and list all the characteristics of them that you can draw from this chapter.

3. Luke 24:36–53.
List all the parallels you can find between this passage and Acts 1.

4. Acts 5:17–41.
What is said about the Holy Spirit in this passage? Make a list of everything in this passage that indicates that the disciples are living in the fullness of the Holy Spirit.

The Evidence That the Holy Spirit Has Come

The results of the infilling of the Holy Spirit

QUICKENING YOUR THINKING

1. What do you think is the evidence of the baptism of the Holy Spirit?

_____

_____

_____

2. What is the biblical evidence that supports your position?

_____

_____

_____

WHAT WE HAVE ALREADY SEEN

In our previous study we saw how the coming of the Holy Spirit was God's solution to the two major problems facing the disciples. Problem one was about whether an intimate relationship with God would be available, and problem two was the self-centeredness of the disciples. When God came to baptize (i.e., cleanse) the disciples from their self-centeredness (problem two), then it was possible for God's full presence to come so the disciples might know Him in a more intimate way than ever before (problem one). The freeing of the disciples from the tyranny of self-will liberates them to be available for an even closer relationship with the Triune God. Purifying them of their self-interest makes it possible for them to be filled with the presence and heart of God.

These two major things that happen on the day of Pentecost, i.e., purity from self-centeredness (the baptism of the Holy Spirit) and the full presence of the Holy God (the infilling of the Holy Spirit), occur simultaneously. They both take place when the Spirit comes upon the group in the upper room. The combination of these two things happening in the lives of these believing Christians leads to other results. Before we come to these other effects of the coming of the Spirit, it is important to note that the other results come because of these two primary things (the baptism and infilling of the Holy Spirit). When believers are cleansed of their independent self-will and filled with the whole presence of the Spirit of God, this work of God is then expressed in four major ways. We may call them four evidences that the Spirit has come in His fullness. Let's look at each of them in turn.

THE RESULTS OF THE FULL PRESENCE OF GOD AND OF PURITY FROM SELF-WILL

Turn in your Bible to Acts 2:1–47 and read through it carefully.

1. THE RESULTS IN EFFECTIVE MINISTRY

✜ THE PROBLEM OF LIMITED SERVANT MINISTRY

Jesus' last evening with the disciples shows that although they have been in ministry with Him for some time, there is a limit to their willingness to give of themselves to others. They do not have full servant hearts, so they will not serve one another or Jesus if that means taking the role of a slave. They do not mind doing ministry which advances themselves or gives them positions of power and authority, but none of them wants a ministry which is sacrificial or behind the scenes.

✜ THE PROMISE OF THE SOLUTION: A MINISTRY OF SELF-DENIAL

When Jesus begins to talk about the Holy Spirit coming to solve their problem, He relates the Spirit's work to one area of ministry, i.e., witnessing. Witnessing or sharing one's faith with others can be a very daunting experience. The reason for this is that a disciple never knows the reaction he will get, and sometimes the reaction may be hostile, as it was for Jesus. The basic issue is whether or not a disciple is willing to sacrifice his feelings, reputation, and perhaps even life, in order to do something for other people. Jesus indicates that when the Spirit comes, there will be an empowering to be this kind of witness for Him in the world (John 15:26–27).

Restate His promise in this regard in Acts 1:8.

_____

_____

_____

_____

✜ THE PRAYER FOR THE SOLUTION: AN ENABLING FOR MINISTRY LIKE THAT OF JESUS

When Jesus prays for the disciples' full sanctification, He immediately follows His petition with the declaration that He is sending them into the world in the same way that He has been sent into the world (John 17:17–18). He clearly is sending them into the world to do the same kinds of ministry which He has been doing and has trained them to do. This will be a ministry of witnessing, preaching, teaching, making disciples, serving people, and meeting spiritual and physical needs (Matthew 4:18–28).

Jesus' prayer for the disciples' sanctification is part of His prayer for the disciples' enablement to do this ministry to others in a way in which they have not done before: with a servant heart. He would like for them to be in ministry to other people with the same sacrificial spirit He has had in ministry to them (e.g., washing their feet).

✜ THE SOLUTION REALIZED: SPIRIT ENABLED, SELF-GIVING MINISTRY

The fullness of the Spirit brings an enablement for sacrificial ministry to others. Jesus promised the disciples they would have power to be witnesses unto Him (Acts 1:8).

What evidence do you see in Acts 2 that the fullness of the Spirit has made this a reality?

_____

_____

_____

_____

What other enablement of the disciples is implied for other forms of ministry? Focus on Acts 2:42–45.

_____

_____

_____

_____

When the Holy Spirit comes, Peter, speaking for the others, stands up and preaches the gospel of Christ with a powerful anointing (Acts 2:14–39). The disciples who have been hiding behind closed doors for fear of the Jews are now enabled to boldly proclaim Christ in the marketplace. This means they are making themselves vulnerable to opposition in order to minister to other people, a sacrifice they have not been willing to make up to this time.

If the problem of the disciples has been a lack of a servant heart (with the result that they have been limited in ministry), the solution has to be a fuller enablement by the Spirit for self-giving ministry to other people. Whereas the problem focuses on self-protection and self-interest, the solution is seen in a willingness to put oneself at risk in ministry to other people. The proclamation of the Word in a public manner places the disciples in a position of jeopardy (2:14–40), and their sacrificial investment in new believers to make them disciples is certainly a costly giving of themselves (2:42–47). The early church's service to one another through the sharing of goods is also a sacrificial giving up of resources in which the disciples are leading others. In the Gospels the disciples are limited in the ministry which they are willing to do. Beginning in Acts 2, there is a greater ability as well as a greater willingness to minister through God's Spirit to others in a variety of ways.

It is worth noting that while occasionally there are miracles and healings done throughout the book of Acts, apparently the normal enablement of the Spirit relates to the "ordinary" ministry of witnessing, preaching, teaching, discipleship, and service. Marginal happenings never become central in the life of the apostles of the early church.

✢ THE SYMBOL FOR SPIRIT-ENABLED MINISTRY

What is the symbol of this witnessing ministry to others as it is described in Acts 2:1–13?

_____

_____

If speaking in other tongues is the symbol, what is the reality to which it is pointing? To put it another way, what capacity for ministry is being implied by this miracle of speaking in tongues?

_____

_____

There is a great deal of discussion about the relationship of speaking in tongues to the coming of the Spirit. In this context there are several options for understanding the phrase "speaking in tongues." It may mean either (1) speaking in an unknown tongue, or (2) speaking in a private prayer language, or (3) speaking in a known foreign language.

Which do you think is the correct interpretation?

_____

_____

What is the evidence to support your conclusion?

_____

_____

_____

_____

Two interesting words are used to describe this speaking in "other tongues." In verses 4 and 11, the Greek word _glossais_, is used. It is the word from which we get _glossalalia._ The other word is _dialecto,_ from which we get our English word _dialect._ This is used in verses 6 and 7, and it refers to languages or dialects which people understand. What do you think are the implications of these two words both being used in this context?

_____

_____

_____

_____

The fact that these two words are used interchangeably in 2:4–11 makes it clear that the speaking in "other tongues" means that they are speaking known foreign languages that are understood by people from a variety of different locations and language groups. How many countries (and therefore language groups) are mentioned in the story?

_____

_____

What do the people from these many different places indicate was the purpose of this miracle of tongues?

_____

_____

A careful reading of the text indicates that this phenomenon is a miracle of communication God has provided by giving those filled with the Spirit the power to speak another language to communicate the "mighty works of God" (2:11). There does not seem to be room here for interpreting "speaking in tongues" as either speaking in an unknown (ecstatic utterance) tongue or as a private prayer language.

Since the phenomenon of tongues has often been connected with the coming of the Holy Spirit, two other observations may be helpful. The first has to do with the question of Jesus and speaking in tongues. Can you think of an occasion where tongues appear in the life or ministry of Jesus or a place where He specifically talks about this phenomenon? If you are not able to recall any occasion where tongues is connected with Jesus in the Gospels, do not feel bad. There are none. What do you think are the implications of this for the lives of disciples of Jesus?

_____

_____

_____

The life and teaching of Jesus indicate that He has come to clarify for us every significant aspect of our spiritual lives and every experience that we need to relate to God. He both models what we need and directs His disciples in their own experience of the Triune God. Everything else they need for their walk with God He addresses (e.g., repentance, faith, prayer, handling the Word, discipleship, fullness of the Spirit, relationship with other disciples, etc.). If speaking in tongues were an essential ingredient for the spiritual life of the disciples of Jesus, it is hard to understand why there is no mention of this by Him or illustration of it in His own life.

We also observe that (apart from Acts 10 and 19) the question of tongues only appears one other time throughout the entire New Testament. It comes in the midst of Paul's dealing with the multiple problems of the church at Corinth. In the middle of his discussion of the role of occasional gifts of the Spirit, the tongues issue arises (Corinthians 12). He then addresses this problem in more detail as a specific area that was troubling the church (1 Corinthians 14). The fact that this issue is not addressed in any other epistle of the New Testament should probably caution us that this is not a central issue for the experience of Christians in the New Testament church.

While a detailed study of Paul's discussion of speaking in tongues in 1 Corinthians can be found in a different context (see Coppedge and Ury, _A Workbook on Spiritual Gifts_, The Barnabas Foundation) a preliminary word about interpreting this passage may be in order. The standard rule for interpreting scripture is that the clear passages in scripture interpret the unclear. You do not take a highly symbolic and debatable passage from Ezekiel or Revelation to interpret straightforward statements in scripture from Isaiah or Romans. The clearest always interprets that which is less clear. Using this principle, it is obvious that the clearest passage about tongues in the New Testament is in Acts 2. These references to tongues are about speaking in known foreign languages. The implication is that this understanding of speaking in tongues should be a major factor in helping understand the role of speaking in tongues in the Corinthian church. More digging on this will have to come in additional study.

In summary of our discussion of effective ministry as an evidence of the coming of the Spirit, we may say that the implication of this symbol of tongues is that God is enabling people to communicate His word to people who need to respond to Him. Tongues is the symbol of the empowering of God to proclaim His word to people.

2. THE RESULTS IN RELATIONSHIPS

✢ THE PROBLEM IN RELATIONSHIPS

The difficulty we have seen among the disciples is their lack of self-giving love toward one another. Because they are protecting their own interests, they are not willing to attend to the needs of others. There is too much focus upon themselves. They have friendships which are close, but they do not have any sacrificial commitment to one another's best interests.

✣ THE PROMISE OF THE SOLUTION: SELF-GIVING LOVE

Jesus exhorts them to love one another in the same way He has loved them, i.e., sacrificially (John 13:34–35). When He begins to discuss the role of the Holy Spirit, He implies that when the Spirit comes, the Spirit will provide an enablement for the disciples to love each other with the same self-giving love which Jesus has for them (John 15:12, 17, 26–27).

✣ THE PRAYER FOR THE SOLUTION: ONENESS OF SPIRIT

When Jesus prays for their sanctification, He desires for the disciples to be one with each other as well as one with Him, implying a oneness of will controlling the disciples and bonding them to one another in Him. He is also praying that the love which He has experienced from the Father may be in them for one another (John 17:26).

✣ THE SOLUTION REALIZED: SURRENDER OF SELF-WILL

As the disciples wait together for the coming of the Holy Spirit, what evidence do you see that they are committing themselves in a deeper way to each other? What happens while they are waiting for the Holy Spirit that makes them ready for a stronger commitment to each other (Acts 1:14–26)?

_____

_____

_____

_____

After Jesus gives the disciples directions, they all return together to the upper room to seek the promise of the Father. They find themselves there for seven days "devoting themselves to prayer" (1:14). In this context there does not appear to be any rivalry among the eleven when they go to choose the twelfth apostle. Peter challenges the group to make a choice to replace Judas, but it is the group that puts forward Joseph and Matthias. They pray together to seek God's mind about whom He has chosen (1:21–25). There does not seem to be the self-seeking which we noticed in the Gospels.

When Peter stands up to preach on the day of Pentecost, it specifically mentions that he was standing "with the eleven," implying that he was speaking for the group, with the support of the whole group. They seem to be working in ministry together. This is also suggested in what they begin to do for the new believers after the tremendous response on the day of Pentecost (Acts 2:42–47).

Perhaps the chief indication that the disciples are looking after the interests of the whole body rather than their own interests comes in the life of Peter. In the early chapters of the book of Acts, he obviously is the leader of the disciples and of the church. However, when the great Jerusalem Council meets in Acts 15, Peter is present, but James, the brother of Jesus, is chairing the meeting. Peter does not hold on to his position of authority, nor does he insist on retaining his status in leadership. Apparently, he has been set free by the apostles for wider ministry.

The evidence indicates that when the Spirit comes in His fullness, the purifying of self-interest liberates individuals to be supportive of one another. They no longer have to protect themselves or their positions. They are free to serve God and other disciples and thus join with others in ministry to the world.

3. THE RESULTS IN GODLY THINKING

✢ THE PROBLEM OF SELF-CENTERED THINKING

The disciples struggle with the problem of their self-orientation. This means they view other people and circumstances through the lens of their own self-interests. They are not willing to serve each other or Jesus because they are looking out for themselves. Their self-will clouds their ability to think about sacrificial service to other people in the same way God thinks about serving people. They just cannot see or think about others through God's eyes or God's mind.

✢ THE PROMISE OF THE SOLUTION: THE SPIRIT WHO BRINGS TRUTH

When Jesus begins to talk about a solution, He describes the Holy Spirit as the Spirit of truth (John 14:17). He is looking for the Spirit to do a fuller work in their minds, so the truth of God will sink deeply into their understanding. The Spirit will bring to their remembrance the things which Jesus spoke to them, and He will also be a guide to all other truth which they need to know (John 14:26; 16:13). The work of the Spirit from Jesus' perspective is inexorably bound up with truth and a right understanding of the way God works.

✢ THE PRAYER FOR THE SOLUTION: SANCTIFICATION IS IN THE TRUTH

When Jesus begins to pray for God to sanctify the disciples, it is a sanctification according to the truth which God has revealed through His Word. The Word of God is both the source of truth and standard for truth. Therefore, it is the Word which forms the basis of right thinking for all disciples. Jesus has taught the disciples to base their thinking on the Word of God as given in the Old Testament (Matt. 5:17–18) and then on His way of thinking which will be the foundation of the New Testament (Matt. 7:24–29). He prays that there will be a work of the Spirit through sanctification which will help them more clearly understand the truth. Only when they are free from their self-centeredness will they be free to think the thoughts of a holy God.

✢ THE SOLUTION REALIZED: THINKING WITHOUT A SELF-CENTERED ORIENTATION

When the Holy Spirit fills disciples, He fills them with the full presence of a holy God. Part of this fullness has to do with His full control of their thinking. He desires to come and take full charge of their minds and therefore their perspective on the world. When they surrender their self-interests and their way of looking at life and people from their own self-centeredness, they are then free to think about things from God's perspective and see people as God sees them.

The first illustration of the change in the disciples' thinking comes in Peter's view of a suffering Messiah. Do you remember Peter's reaction to Jesus' statement about His role as Messiah that would include suffering and death? How would you describe Peter's response in Mark 8:31–33?

Why do you believe he responded in this way?

_____

_____

How does Peter's description of God's way of working through Jesus differ from this in Acts 2:22–23?

_____

_____

A comparison of evidence indicates that there was a time when Peter rejected any concept of a Messiah coming to suffer and die (Mark 8:32), because he was hoping for a different kind of Messiah. At that point Peter's thinking was shaped by his own interest in a position that would give him status, so he was looking for a Messiah who could give him responsibility and authority over others.

After the Spirit comes, Peter stands up to preach and shares about the suffering and death of Christ as part of God's plan and purposes for Jesus (Acts 2:23). Later in Acts (3:18) and also in Peter's first epistle (1 Peter 2:19–24; 3:13–4a), he declares that suffering and sacrifice are part of God's principles for accomplishing His purposes in the world through the Messiah and through His disciples. Peter's thinking has shifted from understanding God's work as something to be done primarily by power, to an understanding that God works primarily through sacrifice and suffering.

Another illustration of a shift in the disciples' thinking can be seen in their vision for the world. Can you think of a place in the Gospels where the disciples express any concern for those who are not a part of the Jewish nation?

_____

_____

What indications do you find in Acts 2 that the apostles are convinced that the gospel is now available for everyone anywhere?

_____

_____

In the Gospels there is a noticeable lack of concern for the Gentile world, but immediately after Pentecost, the disciples begin to share the gospel, proclaiming that this is available to all peoples anywhere (Acts 2:17, 21, 39). For the first time, they are thinking from God's perspective about the whole world, including non-Hebrews.

When the Spirit comes, one of the results is thinking more clearly the way God thinks. This is due primarily to a surrender of one's own self-centered perspective, so a disciple is liberated to think God's thoughts and understand people and circumstances from His point of view.

✣ SYMBOLIC LANGUAGE: THE WORD PENTECOST

Thinking differently is related to the promise God gave in the Old Testament that the fullness of the New Covenant would bring "a law written on the heart" (Jer. 31:33). The symbolic language which indicates a new, fuller way of thinking God's thoughts is in the description of the coming of the Spirit on the very day of Pentecost. We have already seen that _Pentecost_ is the second major festival in the Jewish year. Sometimes called the

Feast of Weeks, Pentecost is the celebration of the giving of the torah at Mt. Sinai. It is a time to rejoice in the establishment of Israel as the people of God, and the giving of the content of the Old Covenant on how to live with a holy God.

The experience of Israel at Mt. Sinai is clearly the birthday of the Old Testament church, and the giving of the law/torah was designed to help the people of God understand how to live with this God and serve Him. The coming of the Holy Spirit on the very day of Pentecost symbolizes the birth of the New Testament church. Appropriately, God's Spirit writes the law on their hearts and begins to help these disciples think like a holy God thinks. The Word of God is no longer just external, i.e., on tablets of stone; it has now been written on the hearts of believers. The coming of the Spirit brings an internalization of the mind of God as well as the heart of God.

4. THE RESULTS IN GODLY CHARACTER

✛ THE PROBLEM OF UN-CHRISTLIKE CHARACTER

The character problem of self-interest in the disciples keeps them from reflecting the selfless heart of Jesus. Instead of His self-giving nature, there is a self-protecting nature, which still is a part of who they are. Instead of looking out for the interests of God and other people, they are looking out for their own interests. We have seen this expressed in several ways.

First, their ungodly character is reflected in their unwillingness to fully submit to the whole will of God in every area of their lives. They are struggling with submission. Judas backs up on Jesus, and Peter goes back and forth. In the garden of Gethsemane, all of the disciples deny Jesus and refuse to identify with Him in order to protect themselves.

Second, none of the disciples love each other enough to take the servant place which Jesus is willing to do. There is a lack of sacrificial love which is unlike the character of Jesus.

The heart of the matter is that being unlike Jesus means that they are not fully holy as God is holy. Their lack of total submission and unconditional love make them unlike a holy God, who through the person of Jesus has shown us how He fully gives Himself and loves unconditionally.

✛ THE PROMISE OF THE SOLUTION: THE AGENT OF A HOLY GOD

When Jesus starts to talk about the coming of the Spirit, He begins to challenge the disciples to make a choice of complete submission and therefore full obedience, so the Spirit can have full possession of their lives (John 14:15–16). Coupled with this is an exhortation to love as He loves and to fully give themselves to one another (John 13:34–35). The solution will be wrapped up with the coming of the Holy Spirit.

✛ THE PRAYER FOR THE SOLUTION: SANCTIFICATION OF CHARACTER

When Jesus prays for the sanctification of their character, He is concerned that their oneness of will involves a complete submission to the full will of God (John 17:22–23). He wants them to know in themselves the unconditional love the Father has had for Him (John 17:26). He prays to the Holy Father that they might be made holy, i.e., sanctified, in oneness of will and therefore oneness of character (John 17:11, 17).

✛ THE SOLUTION REALIZED: TRANSFORMATION OF CHARACTER AT PENTECOST

When Jesus leaves the disciples, they immediately begin to make the choices to submit to His will for their lives.

What evidence have you already seen in Acts 1 of this choice to fully obey/submit?

_____

_____

_____

_____

The disciples return to the upper room to wait for the promise of the Father, not knowing how long that will take. Their submission is seen in their waiting more than a week and seeking the whole will of God, including His direction for the replacement of Judas (Acts 1:24–25).

After Pentecost

As soon as the Spirit comes, the evidence of a character wholly controlled by God's character is seen when the disciples start to obey Jesus' command to make disciples of all nations. They begin to fulfill the first part of the Great Commission by a proclamation of the Word of God (Acts 2:14–39), and then they initiate the discipleship training as soon as people start responding to the gospel (2:42ff). Jesus told them to go and make disciples. As soon as the Spirit fills them, they begin doing exactly what he instructed them to do. This is the kind of full obedience He has been looking for.

We are also struck by the fact that all the disciples are willing to be identified with Jesus, even if this identification puts their own lives in jeopardy. When Peter and John are brought before the Sanhedrin, they boldly declare that salvation is available through no one else but Jesus (Acts 4:4–12, 19–20). This is a marked contrast to their fear of being identified with Jesus on their last night with Him. There is a new love and identification with Jesus in them.

You also see this full submission to the whole will of God a little later in Peter, when the Lord challenges him to go to the Gentiles (Acts 10). All his prejudices are against this kind of ministry, but he is willing to do what God wants and therefore goes, submitting to the will of God.

✛ THE SYMBOLIC TERMS RELATED TO HOLY CHARACTER

▲ Kingdom of God

The symbolic language connected to this full submission to the whole will of God is the phrase "the kingship of God." Jesus spends forty days appearing occasionally to the disciples after His resurrection, "speaking of the kingdom of God" (Acts 1:3). The word for _kingdom_ really is the word for _kingship_. It refers, not to a political, economic, or geographical kingdom, but to the _reign of God_ in the lives of people.

When the disciples raise the question about restoring the kingdom (Acts 1:6), why does Jesus respond with a promise about the coming of the Holy Spirit? How are the "kingship of God" and the coming of the Holy Spirit related?

_____

_____

_____

_____

Jesus responds to the disciples' question with a promise of the Holy Spirit coming upon them. He is not ignoring their question. He is trying to show them that God's full kingship in their lives is related to God's coming through His Holy Spirit to take full possession of them. This kind of kingship is only possible if they have fully surrendered their lives and are willing to be wholly obedient in every area of their lives. This is the choice they are making in Acts 1, and when the Spirit comes it is clear that God does have a full kingly reign in their lives. This means that the complete submission of their wills to the Holy Spirit makes it possible to reflect the character of Jesus.

▲ Love from the Father

A second result in their character is an impartation of sacrificial love expressed as self-giving love. The word *love* itself is not mentioned in Acts 2. Is there in the narrative any indication of a different level of love appearing in the disciples?

_____

_____

_____

_____

The story does indicate that the disciples have been changed. Although they did not love Jesus enough to be identified with Him on their last night together, on the day of Pentecost this new love provides a motivation to boldly identify with Him, even if it costs them their lives. They stand up to share the gospel (Acts 2). They teach about Jesus (Acts 3). They boldly present Christ to the Sanhedrin (Acts 4:8–22; 5:17–21). We do not see any protecting of themselves, but rather a willingness to sacrifice themselves, just as Jesus had done for them.

The symbolic language related to this kind of self-giving love is described in terms of Jesus' relationship to God as Father. Where do you see references to this family language that describes God as Father? Check 1:1–11; 2:29–36.

_____

_____

When Jesus tells the disciples not to depart from Jerusalem, He enjoins them "to wait for the promise of the Father" (1:4). When they ask about God's kingly rule, Jesus responds with the discussion of the Father being the One who has fixed the proper time to exercise His authority (1:7). Peter understands this very well, so when he is preaching on the day of Pentecost, he talks about Jesus being at the right hand of God, "having received from the Father the promise of the Holy Spirit, he has poured out this which you see and hear" (Acts 2:33).

The language of God as the Father of Jesus and the spiritual Father for the disciples, sets the tone for understanding unconditional, self-giving love. It is a family concept. In the language of the home, God sets the standard of the character He wants to see in disciples. He is looking for children who have come to maturity and are reflecting His own nature and image. God wants to see people who love as He does, i.e., love as Jesus loves, and who are therefore willing to lay down their lives for others. After Pentecost this love, reflecting Jesus Himself, fills the disciples. It is the character of love; it is the character of Jesus.

Perhaps the character of God is most fully depicted in the description of His holiness. Jesus promises the Holy Spirit will make the disciples holy, and then Peter tells us that Jesus himself, who is the "Holy One" (Acts 2:27), has sent the Holy Spirit from the Father (2:33).

When the disciples are filled with the Holy Spirit, they are filled with the Father, Son, and Spirit, all of whom are holy at their essence. When they are fully possessed by the Spirit of this holy God, they become holy as He is holy, and then they reflect His character.

Since character really is controlled by the will, it is the full submission of the will, i.e., the total surrender of self-will, that makes it possible for God to reflect His holiness in the lives of the disciples. Thus the question of character ultimately takes us back to the issue of the surrender of self-will to the full will of a holy God. When God comes to take charge of their character, He is then in a position to shape their ministry, their relationships, and their thinking in a way He could not do before.

◆ REVIEWING THE RESULTS

Having walked through the biblical materials about the results of the coming of the Spirit, we need to review them to keep perspective. We have tried to look at the coming of the Spirit in Acts 1–2 in light of the larger context of Jesus' preparing disciples for this event, beginning back in John 13. We have identified two major problems the disciples have, namely, the problem of intimacy with God and the problem of self-centeredness within themselves. Then we have seen how Jesus prepared the way for dealing with both of these in His teaching the disciples (John 14–16) and His prayer for their sanctification (John 17). This means that what happens in His final preparation of the disciples (Acts 1) and in the coming of the Spirit (Acts 2) are all related to a larger picture. Now we can understand more fully what is really involved when the Spirit comes, and this allows us to more accurately discern what the real indications of His presence are.

In the outline of our previous study, we focused upon the infilling of the Holy Spirit, representing the full presence of a holy God filling disciples. This was followed by a discussion of the baptism of the Holy Spirit, describing the cleansing or purification from self-centeredness within disciples. In this study we have focused our attention on the results that flow from these two (infilling and baptism in the Spirit) in ministry, relationships, thinking, and character.

As we review this combination of elements, we will change the order of discussion. We are now going to look at this combination of factors in terms of the logical progression of what takes place in the individual when all of these things happen. The focus here is not so much on chronology (because much of this happens at the same time) as it is on a logical explanation of the way God works as we try to understand the effects of the Spirit's coming in His fullness.

1. PURIFICATION FROM SELF-WILL

It is the "baptism of the Holy Spirit" which describes the cleansing of the heart from self-centeredness. It is this cleansing or purification, symbolized by the word *baptism*, which describes the surrender of the will to God and the resulting purification of a self-orientation from a disciples' life. This is the negative side of this experience in the sense that something has to go before God's full presence can come. What has to go is the independent self-will. Thus there is a putting aside of one's own way, and this is often described in scripture with cleansing or purification language. In this case "the baptism of the Holy Spirit" describes this phenomenon. The self-centeredness of a disciple's life is washed away.

2. THE FULLNESS OF GOD'S PRESENCE

This purifying of the life from self-will makes it possible for God to assume full control of the will and therefore the life. This means that God can be fully present in a person's life, and it is the "infilling of the Holy Spirit" which represents this fullness of the presence of a holy God.

This full presence of God through His Spirit results in His full possession of an individual. Because God now completely controls one's will, He fully controls one's life, i.e., He fully possesses all of a person. Without the surrender of the will and self-interest, God's full controlling presence cannot take possession of a person's life. This is what "being filled with the Holy Spirit" (Acts 2:4) is all about. We may visualize it in this way:

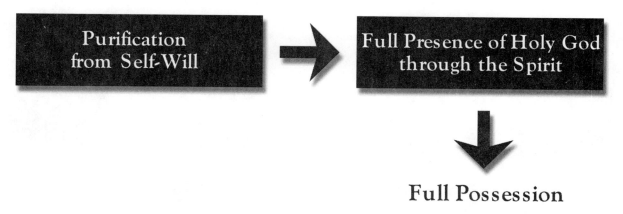

3. SANCTIFICATION OF CHARACTER

The surrender of self-will and the full presence of the Holy Spirit come together to make a disciple holy through the transforming power of God. This is an internal transformation causing one's character to reflect the character of a holy God. This subjective change of character which makes a person holy (i.e., sanctifies them) is expressed primarily in two ways.

The first expression of a sanctified character is full submission and therefore full obedience to God. This is only possible when the will is fully surrendered so that then God can take full possession of it with His presence. This possession of the life will be expressed in character in terms of full obedience, leading to righteous living. One is able to walk victoriously and according to God's standard of righteousness because of this transformation of character by the Spirit.

The second expression of sanctified character is in the sacrificial love of a holy God flowing from a purified heart. Because a disciple does not first love himself but now first loves God, God infuses him with a self-giving love which represents His own character. The sanctification of character then, comes out of the purification of self-will and the full presence of the Holy Spirit. It looks like this:

4. TRANSFORMATION OF THINKING

The purification from self-centeredness, plus the full presence of the Holy Spirit, plus the sanctification of character, leads to a transformation of thinking. Part of making a disciple holy has to do not only with the character centered in the heart, but with the thinking centered in the mind. By setting aside self-interest, the disciple is free to think as God thinks. While the content of thinking must still be developed as one lives with the Word of God and continues to get God's principles firmly fixed in the mind, there is a way of thinking that is now possible because one can see and understand from God's perspective. Here is how godly thinking emerges:

5. HOLY RELATIONSHIPS

When a life is cleansed of self-interest and the Spirit of God takes full possession of an individual, this not only changes the character and thinking, but it purifies all personal relationships. Now the relationships with other disciples, and even unbelievers, is not tainted with self-concern. Thus it is possible to relate to people as God would relate to them, i.e., with a self-giving, sacrificial spirit. Now one can love people as God loves them and minister to them as God would. The results are purified relationships and a bonded relationship of love with other disciples of Jesus. The connection flows like this:

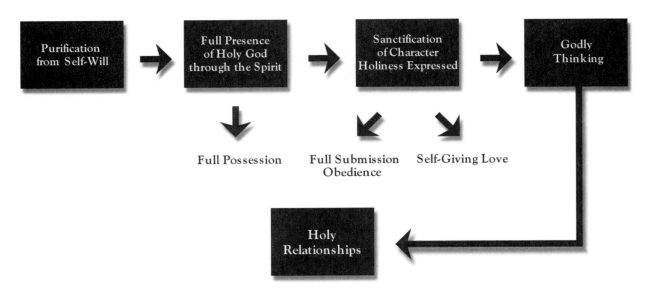

6. Ministry in the Holy Spirit

The last effect of the coming of the Spirit is fruitful ministry in the Spirit. Because a disciple has been purified of self-will and now enjoys being fully possessed by the Holy Spirit, and because his character is being transformed to reflect the character of this holy God, his thinking now is more like the thinking of a Holy God, his relationships are purified, and it is possible for him to minister to other people like Jesus would minister to them. **What a disciple does for God in the lives of others is not the first effect of the coming of the Holy Spirit, it is the last one.** While this service is a part of God's desire and a natural result of the Spirit's full control of our lives, ministry must be related to a purified heart, the full presence of God, a transformed character, thinking like the mind of God, and bonded relationships with other disciples. This is the way Jesus did ministry, and this is the way He wants His disciples to do it.

It is interesting to notice that as soon as the disciples are empowered for ministry on the day of Pentecost, they begin to be obedient to Jesus' commission to go and make other disciples. Peter begins with evangelism, in an outreach to unbelievers (Acts 2:14–41). Then the disciples all begin the second half of the Great Commission by training new believers to be disciples (Acts 2:42–47). In order to make disciples, they are involved in preaching, teaching, service, and care to others. Their focus is training disciples like Jesus did. From Jesus' perspective, one key ingredient for being a disciple-maker is coming into an experience where God has full possession of one's life through the infilling of the Holy Spirit. For the disciples, fruit in the lives of other people does not come without the connection to these other effects of God working in them through the fullness of His presence.

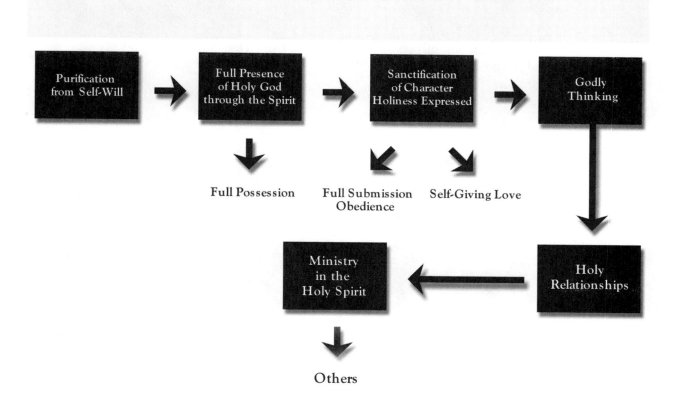

As you review the effects of the coming of the Holy Spirit, you will want to ask God to reveal whether all of these are characteristic of your own life. If there are some which are not present, then you will want to ask for the fullness of His sanctifying presence to make you the disciple and disciple-maker which He longs for you to be.

> ### Memory Verses
> Acts 1:8 and Acts 2:41–42

Additional Passages for Study

You may wish to study some of these passages more fully during the Word portion of your devotional time.

1. Acts 2.

Make an outline of Peter's message and the response.

2. Acts 2:14–47.

How does this passage relate to the parts of the Great Commission in Matthew 28:19–20?

3. Ezekiel 36:16–38.

How many of the six effects of the coming of the Holy Spirit (on the previous diagram) can you find described ahead of time by the prophet?

4. Luke 3:21–22, 4:1–5:11

How many of the six effects of the coming of the Holy Spirit can you see modeled in the life of Jesus?

The Coming of the Spirit After Pentecost

Understanding the work of the Holy Spirit in Acts

THE SPIRIT AND THE BOOK OF ACTS

The book of Acts is undoubtedly the most complete historical and experiential account of the Spirit-filled lives of the apostles. There are no less than ten references to lives filled with the Spirit which include a variety of places and contexts. Based upon adequate rules of interpretation, a proper understanding of the passages which come after Acts 2 must relate to Pentecost in some comparative way. Remember the basic interpretive rule: the clear passages interpret the unclear ones. Acts 2 is certainly the clearest passage about the coming of the Spirit and the resulting effects on the disciples.

The interpretation of the Spirit-filled life in the book of Acts must also relate to what precedes it as well as the explanations and implications which come after it in the early church. It is easy to see why the interpretation of these passages is so important. If one raises theological or experiential barriers concerning the experience of the fullness of the Spirit in the early church, then one has already constricted what the epistles can say about the life of holiness.

QUICKENING YOUR THINKING:

1. Do you remember in the Gospels what is the most frequently used phrase pertaining to the relationship between the Holy Spirit and the individual believer? (Check Matt. 3:11, Mark 1:8, Luke 3:16, John 1:33)

_____

_____

2. Can you think of times in the early church, from the book of Acts or the epistles, when a picture similar to Acts 2 is used to describe the presence of the Holy Spirit among the people of God? List them below.

_____

_____

3. What do you think those experiences represent? Salvation? Sanctification? Both?

_____

_____

WHAT IS BEFORE US

The best way to approach this study is simply to compare and contrast the various passages in the book of Acts which describe the spiritual experiences of the early disciples and interpret them accordingly.

◆ THE DISCIPLES AT PENTECOST

⊹ REVIEW ACTS 2:1–4

List the facts as you find them here. Who is involved? Is there any indication of their background or spiritual condition before Pentecost? How do you interpret this occurrence in light of our studies in the Gospels? Is this an experience of initial salvation or one of full sanctification?

_____

_____

_____

⊹ IMPLICATIONS OF OUR PREVIOUS STUDIES

Basic interpretive laws of scripture include the often used logical progression which comes from an introductory or preparatory statement. The Gospels have given us a picture of the disciples which is less than exemplary. We know that the church will soon go into all the world. So something has yet to happen in the individual lives of the disciples as they approach the Great Commission in light of their own strength. Without a power from outside their lives, nothing they attempt will bear fruit.

Past lessons have clarified the fact that the disciples were believers before Pentecost, and there is a very strong probability that Jesus' prayer for them to be sanctified (John 17:17) is fulfilled here. Any other interpretation of this passage raises the thorny issue of the possibility of an unfulfilled prayer by our Lord Jesus for the lives of His own followers. It is interesting to note that those who claim that sanctification occurs at the point of death (because they think it is impossible to have true victory over sin prior to that moment) never mention that the future tense of the word "to sanctify" never occurs in the New Testament. Conversion, justification, reconciliation, and sanctification are an expectation by Jesus and the authors of the New Testament as a possibility here and now (cf. Luke 24:49; Acts 1:5, 8).

Our previous studies present a strong case for the full sanctification of the apostles and others in the upper room. This is especially true in light of the changed lives of the apostles which ensue from this upper room experience. They experience and express something more than power for external ministry; there has been an internal transformation.

◆ THE OFFER TO THE THREE THOUSAND

Turn in your Bible to Acts 2:38–47 and read carefully.

List the facts as you find them here. Who is involved? Is there any indication of their background or spiritual condition? How do you interpret this occurrence in light of the experience of those in the upper room? Is it the same or different?

_____

_____

_____

As you try to discern whether this event relates to the conversion or the sanctification of the people present, what are the possibilities for interpreting the relationship of the Holy Spirit to this group?

_____

_____

_____

✦ LOOKING AT THE OPTIONS

We are told that the group addressed included Jerusalem Jews and other devout God-fearers from neighboring lands, which probably indicates various levels of spiritual understanding. Peter's biblical and theological preaching (2:14–36) implies they had a deep awareness of Israel's history and prophecy and were looking for the consummation of Israel's faith in an expectant manner. Note that when Peter responds to their question about what they should do in light of the convicting work of the Holy Spirit, he uses two key phrases which have defined the call to commitment and relationship in the Gospels (2:37–38). First, repent and be baptized for forgiveness, and second, receive the gift of the Holy Spirit.

Both of these we have seen are calls to *being*: the work of God's grace in the individual life. All *doing* flows from this reception of God's dynamic work in the soul.

Here are at least four possible interpretations of what happened to these people:

Option 1. This is an experience of initial salvation that includes the receiving of the Spirit in a full sanctifying sense. This option makes basic conversion and the receiving of the fullness of the Spirit in sanctification identical.

Option 2. This is an experience of conversion with the receiving the Spirit in an initial sense. We have earlier referred to the fact that all disciples of Jesus have the Spirit (John 14:16–17). When one enters into a relationship with Jesus, he also receives a new relationship with the Father and the Spirit. Jesus refers to the experience of the new birth as one of being born of the Spirit (John 3:5).

Option 3. This is a conversion experience in some of those present and a "receiving of the Spirit" in the sense of the fullness of the Spirit, i.e., in a sanctifying sense, in others.

Option 4. This is an experience of conversion without receiving the Holy Spirit in the sense of the fullness of Spirit in sanctification at this time. This second part of the offer would be expected at some later time (possibly Acts 4).

Your own study will have indicated that the call to those who heard Peter was to repent and be baptized, indicating the need for an initial salvation experience. The contrast between this group of people and the 120 in the upper room is significant in that the 120 are already clearly believers in Jesus without the need of repentance and baptism for forgiveness in the same way.

Further, if Acts 2:1–4 becomes the basis for helping interpret Acts 2:38, this is strong evidence that those responding to Peter are not receiving the fullness of the Spirit at this time in the same way those did who were in the upper room. This certainly speaks against option one (above) that would make synonymous initial salvation and receiving of the Spirit in the sense of the fullness of the Spirit in sanctification.

Our studies have indicated that the disciples and others in the upper room already had a relationship with the Holy Spirit prior to Pentecost. This means that when the Spirit came upon their lives in Acts 2:4, they received the Holy Spirit in the sense of receiving the fullness of the Spirit in sanctification. Since their experience of salvation (with the initial receiving of the Spirit) was distinct from receiving the fullness of Spirit in sanctification, then it would be natural for Peter to be offering others in his preaching the experience of salvation along with receiving the Holy Spirit in the initial sense rather than in the full, sanctifying sense. This makes option two a real possibility.

It is also possible that in an audience with various levels of faith and relationship to God, some need to come to an initial decision of faith (salvation), while others who are people of vital, living faith may have been ready for receiving the Holy Spirit in the sense of an infilling of the Spirit (sanctification). There is no direct indication that they are filled with the Spirit at this point, so option three is possible but certainly not clearly indicated.

Lastly, it may well be that the response of the people in v. 41 helps interpret the paragraph. "So those who received His Word were baptized, and there were added that day about three thousand souls." This verse suggests that there is a reception of Peter's word by faith, resulting in being baptized and added to the group of believers. There is no direct word that at this point they received the gift of the Holy Spirit.

One way to interpret Peter's invitation to "receive the gift of the Holy Spirit" is to say it includes all of what is available to them under the promises of the New Covenant. It may well be that Peter is saying nothing about any sequence of how this may be received. As they respond in repentance, faith, and baptism, they initially begin a relationship with Jesus. Option four then opens the possibility that some of these are candidates for receiving the fullness of the Spirit at a later time, such as the experience described in Acts 4.

This much is clear. Because there are at least four different possibilities of interpreting this passage, it would not be wise to make this experience a paradigm for understanding any additional "comings" of the Spirit recorded in the Book of Acts. A much safer grid for interpreting further passages would be the clearer event in the upper room (2:1–4).

◆ THE JERUSALEM CHURCH
Turn to Acts 4:31–37 and read carefully.

List the facts as you find them here: Who are the people involved? Is there any indication of their background or spiritual condition?

_____

_____

_____

How do you interpret this occurrence in light of the previous comings of the Spirit in the book? Is this a conversion experience, one of full sanctification, or something else?

_____

_____

_____

✣ What Happens To Some Jewish Christians

Most likely, we have here a group of Jewish Christian believers (see v. 23). Peter and John come from their confrontation with Jewish leadership of the Sanhedrin (Acts 4:5–22). When they are released, they go to their friends and report what had just happened to them. These friends are the ones lifting up their voices in prayer and they are ultimately filled with the Holy Spirit. This company of friends would certainly seem to be fellow believers, and it would be a reasonable inference to assume that many of them had responded to the gospel through Peter's preaching on the day of Pentecost. It may well be we have an example here of some who have come to initial faith on the Pentecost and are now appropriating the second part of Peter's promise (2:38) that they can receive the gift of the fullness of the Spirit.

There is no way to escape the prominence of Spirit-endued power for witness in this chapter (4:8, 31). We find it also in Acts 2:8, 11, as fifteen different languages are used for the proclamation of the Gospel. Peter's first sermon (Acts 2:14–36) comes after the Spirit has descended. His second sermon on the Temple Mount is also an example of this enduement (3:11–26). The boldness of Peter and John before the Sanhedrin (the same group which orchestrated Jesus' death) further indicates the anointing of the Spirit for witness (4:8–22). When Peter reports the encounter with the Sanhedrin, his Christian friends begin to pray for a similar boldness to fall upon them, and it occurs (4:29–33). A desire to think like God thinks and to assist others to do so by witness, proclamation, and teaching is one of the results of the intimacy made possible by the Holy Spirit.

It would seem reasonable to infer that these are persons who have some significant commitment to Christ in their background prior to this experience. When the Spirit comes in sanctifying power, He unleashes a new enablement and boldness to proclaim the truth which bears fruit in an equally powerful way.

"When they had prayed, the place in which they were gathered together was shaken; and they were all filled with the Holy Spirit and spoke the Word of God with boldness" (4:31). This understanding of what is happening in Acts 4 parallels the experience of the disciples in the upper room. It is a picture of believing followers of Jesus who have come to a deeper level of surrender and trust, coupled with the desire to have an empowerment for witness. As a result in both cases, the Spirit fills them and they speak the Word of God with boldness.

◆ THE SAMARITANS
Turn to Acts 8:4–17 and read carefully.

List the facts as you find them here. Who is involved? Is there any indication of their background or spiritual condition?

_____

_____

_____

_____

How do you interpret this occurrence in light of the earlier comings of the Spirit in the book? Is this a conversion experience, one of full sanctification, or something else?

_____

_____

_____

_____

✛ WHAT HAPPENS TO THE SAMARITANS

The Samaritans, you will recall, are half-Jews. They are despised by those who considered their bloodline tainted and their religion cultic. One evidence of the transforming power of the Spirit in the disciples' lives is the willingness to even enter Samaritan territory, much less to have such intimate communion with those they would have been trained to look down on for all of their religious lives.

Note that the Samaritans believe the testimony of Philip and are baptized into an initial experience of redemption (vv. 6, 12).

Write down what these verses indicate about the Samaritans' faith.

Acts 8:6_____

_____

Acts 8:8_____

_____

Acts 8:12_____

_____

Acts 8:14_____

_____

Acts 8:16_____

_____

With all this evidence for their salvation, there is an almost immediate assessment by the leaders in Jerusalem that the Samaritans need to be offered what the disciples have come to know as the Spirit-filled life. This story provides a clear indication of the conversion of the Samaritans, which is neither deficient nor misunderstood (vv. 13–14). To the apostles it is obvious that these persons need to be brought into a fullness of the Spirit as the next phase of their spiritual experience.

The place of the Holy Spirit and power is brought into bold relief by the charlatan, Simon (8:9–24). There is no place in the New Testament where you have a Spirit-filled Christian asking for or offering "power-plays" as Simon did. He is presented here in distinct contrast to those who are truly filled with the humble Holy Spirit. There is a contrast of true power expressed through selfless ministers of the gospel and the abuse of that spiritual vitality when the Spirit has not come to change the motives of spiritual life. Simon is not an example of the Samaritans who are filled with the Spirit. His life is a contrast to a truly sanctified life.

The narrative of the Samaritans seems to fit the pattern established in Acts 2:1–4 in the upper room and followed again in Acts 4. It is the story of some believing Christians who come into a subsequent experience of the fullness of the Spirit in their lives. In all three cases God is doing something more than their experience of initial salvation.

If our study of the disciples and their experience at Pentecost serves as a pattern to interpret the rest of the comings of the Spirit, then these stories in Acts 4 and Acts 8 come as additional illustrations of those believing Christians for whom God does further work in their lives. This is their experience of the coming of the Spirit in His fullness in their lives.

◆ **THE STORY OF PAUL**
Turn to Acts 9:1–18 and read carefully.

List the facts as you find them here. Who is involved? Is there any indication of their background or spiritual condition?

_____

_____

How do you interpret this occurrence in light of the previous comings of the Spirit in the book? Is this Paul's conversion experience, an experience of full sanctification, both, or something else?

_____

_____

_____

✤ WHAT HAPPENS TO PAUL

There is probably no more famous conversion story than that of the Pharisee, Saul, who met the Lord and became the apostle Paul (9:1–9). Ananias, the initially unwilling missionary, is told by God to go and lay hands on Paul that he might be filled with the Holy Spirit (v. 17). It would seem that in this interesting story of an individual conversion, there may be an indication of something deeper transpiring, especially given the ministry which God had planned for Paul (cf. v. 15).

Although we might be able to see a distinction between restored sight (regeneration) and the filling of the Spirit (sanctification, v. 17), there is not enough evidence here to make that assessment unequivocally. Experience shows that the normal sequence of salvation from sins and a revelation of the sin which taints the believers heart takes more time. We cannot wholly disallow that possibility in light of the power of a Holy God, nor the intriguing mix of truth and falsehood at this point in Paul's very unique life and this revelation from Jesus concerning his calling.

We need to take note that this highly trained Jewish scholar asks a question of Jesus on the road that was not solely the result of fear. For a Pharisee of Saul's caliber to ask, "Who are you?" (v. 5) is remarkable (cf. Ananias' usage of the title in vv. 10, 13, 15). We must at least allow the possibility that Saul was converted at this point on the road. Comparing Paul's further explanation of this experience may help shed light also on the conversion-sanctification continuum. He later tells us more about his prayer to the Lord and obedience to His voice (Acts 21:10).

Paul also articulates the full message received on the road from Jesus, where Jesus calls him to offer to the Gentiles forgiveness and sanctification by faith (Acts 26:18).

What is Paul doing for the three days between his experience with Jesus on the Damascus road and the coming of Ananias to pray for him?

_____

_____

What does Ananias' address to Paul suggest about Paul's current spiritual status?

_____

_____

We may well have a situation in which Paul enters into a personal relationship with Jesus on the Damascus road, and then he spends three days fasting and praying about what God desires to do in his own life. The fact that Ananias addresses him as "brother Saul" (v. 17) is suggestive that Ananias understands him already to be a man of faith.

So, there is the possibility that what we have here is a deeply religious person, who, having the basic concepts of the law and righteousness in place, is reconciled to his Redeemer on the road to Damascus and filled with His presence subsequently when Ananias prays for Him.

While we may not have a description of a subsequent experience in Paul's life laid out as clearly for us as it is in some of the stories in Acts, there is little doubt that he did go on to live in the fullness of the Spirit which is so central to all of his major writings.

◆ CORNELIUS AND THE GOD-FEARING GENTILES
Turn to Acts 10:1–11:17 and read carefully.

List the facts as you find them here. Who is involved? Is there any indication of their background or spiritual condition?

_____

_____

_____

How do you interpret this occurrence in light of the previous comings of the Spirit in the book? Is this a conversion experience? Were they believers in God before this? Is this a sanctification experience? A unique blend of salvation and sanctification? Something else?

_____

_____

_____

✜ WHAT HAPPENS TO THE GOD-FEARING GENTILES

In this beautiful story of one of the earliest contacts for Christ with the Gentile world, we have an example of the breadth of the concept of the Spirit's coming. There is no doubt that the emphasis here is on understanding the life of Christ as the basis of one's relationship with God. List the terms you find here that describe their experience:

Acts 10:45_____

_____

Acts 10:46_____

_____

Acts 10:47_____

_____

Acts 10:48_____

_____

Acts 11:1_____

_____

Acts 11:14_____

_____

Acts 11:15_____

_____

Acts 11:16_____

_____

Acts 11:17_____

_____

While there is no reservation at all in interpreting these phrases as initiatory, there seems to be something more at work, which again may not fit into our initial impression of the text. In Peter's further defense of this experience in 15:8–9 he describes two categories: belief in Jesus and cleansing. Note that *cleansing* is a word which is used primarily in scripture for cleansing from moral defilement (cf. Matt. 5:8, 5:48; 2 Cor 7:1; Eph. 5:26; and 1 John 1:7). We have already seen it as part of understanding the baptism of the Spirit in the experience of the twelve (Acts 1:5).

There is the distinct possibility that the normal Christian life in the early church was seen as being in the fullness of the Spirit. If so, it is probable that these God-fearers were seeking Him with all of their hearts and may have come to Him with an unusual openness to all that was available from Jesus, both initial salvation and an indwelling of the Spirit in His sanctifying presence. Here again the meshing of experiences under the aegis of one inclusive, biblical metaphor, such as baptism, is possibly at work. The point is that Peter is focusing on much more than what we often interpret as evangelism. He sees the goal of the Holy Spirit in the believer's life as more than initial reconciliation. The Christian life is a life of a cleansed heart and a blameless conscience (24:16).

Let's take another look at the description of Cornelius throughout the chapter. How is his relationship to God described?

_____

Would you say that he is already a man of significant faith? It certainly seems appropriate to describe him as one who has at least the faith of an Old Testament believer, even though he is living in the New Testament age.

This opens the possibility that Cornelius, representing these Gentile God-fearers, is already a man of such significant faith (cf. vv. 2, 4, 22, 24, 31, 33) that the understanding of Jesus as the source of his salvation and an openness to the fuller sanctifying work of the Spirit comes at the same moment. With this interpretation, the conversion of believers to Christ (in the Old Testament sense) comes with a receptivity to all God has for them, so that their "receiving the Holy Spirit" is a coalescing of salvation and sanctification in a unique way, not seen up to this point in the New Testament church.

◆ THE EPHESIAN GENTILES
Turn to Acts 19:1–7 and read carefully.

List the facts as you find them here. Who is involved? Is there any indication of their background or spiritual condition? You may wish to refer to 18:24–28.

_____

_____

_____

How do you interpret this occurrence in light of the previous comings of the Spirit in the book? Is this an experience of conversion, one of sanctification, or something else?

_____

_____

_____

✛ WHAT HAPPENS TO THE EPHESIAN GENTILES

When Paul arrives at Ephesus, he finds that the disciples there have two significant problems. They do not know about the Holy Spirit nor feel they have "received" Him. Neither have they understood the importance of being baptized in the name of Jesus, knowing only that of John the Baptist. The question is, does this mean they are not believing Christians, or that they are only uninformed believers who need the Holy Spirit as the next step in their lives?

Taking the entire book as our guide here, it is important to note these Ephesian Christians are called "disciples" (19:1). No one is called a "disciple" in Acts who is not a believer in Jesus (cf. 11:26, 29). Their problem very likely stems from the influence of Apollos, who while having been instructed in the way of the Lord and taught accurately about Jesus, knew only the baptism of John (18:24–25). The issue seems to be misunderstanding regarding questions of baptism and the work of the Holy Spirit.

On Paul's arrival, his natural first question for the believers was about their experience of the fullness of the Holy Spirit. When he realizes they do not even understand about the existence of the Spirit, he backs up to their conversion experience and the public witness by baptism. Here he recognizes their ignorance regarding the importance of being baptized in the name of Jesus. His solution therefore is to treat these two things in sequence by first baptizing them in the name of the Lord. Then, as if meeting a second need, he lays hands on them (symbolizing prayer for them) and the Holy Spirit "came upon them" (19:5–6). When the Spirit comes, the experience of the Ephesians is very similar to those at Pentecost and at Caesura (v. 6).

◆ PUTTING IT ALL TOGETHER

✛ THE VARIETY OF LANGUAGE

As you think about the varieties of ways in which the New Testament speaks about salvation, how many come to your mind?

_____

_____

A moment's reflection indicates that God has used a host of ways to talk about this big experience of His saving grace. So we find multiple kinds of language being employed to talk about how God draws people to Himself in regeneration, entering the kingdom, pardon, following Jesus, forgiveness, justification by faith, the new birth, redemption, deliverance, being found, healing, etc. No one of these terms describes everything that happens in the experience of God's saving grace, but each contributes something to the full picture of the way God works when He draws people into a saving relationship with Himself.

The same phenomenon seems to be at work regarding the experience of the fullness of the Spirit. This is a big experience that can not be adequately explained with the use of only one term or phrase.

From memory, can you think of the ways the fullness of the Spirit has been described in our recent studies?

_____

_____

_____

The variety of language scripture uses for this significant experience is indicative of the multiple things God is doing and His desire for us to understand it in more than one way. These are the terms that we have already seen identified:

Does this variety of language help us interpret the experience of the coming of the Spirit? In particular, does it address the issue of whether these experiences are a deeper work of sanctification in the lives of believers or whether or not they may relate only to an initial experience of salvation? The force of our studies through the Gospels and Acts 1–2 certainly seems to connect several of the key words with an experience of sanctification in the lives of believing disciples. This would include the references to sanctify them (John 17:17), the promise of the Father (Acts 1:4), the baptism of the Holy Spirit (Acts 1:5; 11:16), the coming of the Holy Spirit (Acts 1:8; 19:6), and being filled with the Holy Spirit (Acts 2:4; 4:31; 9:17). The flow of stories that connected this language certainly favors the interpretation that this experience is something more than initial conversion for believing disciples.

This understanding of these terms (which are clearer in focus) becomes part of the help we need to interpret the phrases that seem less clear. These less clear terms include the language of receiving the Spirit (Acts 2:38, 8:15, 17; 10:47), the Holy Spirit falling

(10:44; 11:15), the Holy Spirit being poured out (10:45), and the Holy Spirit cleansing hearts by faith (15:8–9). The second set of terms might be interpreted either as the sanctifying work of God in believers or as an experience of initial salvation. The connection with the previous set of terms, however, strongly weighs the evidence toward the second group being also a means of describing the full sanctification of believers through the Spirit.

✛ THE COMINGS OF THE SPIRIT

In addition to the discussion of the variety of language that seems to describe the same experience, how do the multiple descriptions of the coming of the Spirit help us interpret this work of God in the lives of people? Looking collectively at the total group of stories, the basic question is, are these experiences those of full sanctification of believers or do they reflect an initial experience of salvation for unbelievers?

To answer this question, some have wanted to begin with Acts 2:38 and the three thousand pilgrims on the day of Pentecost who responded to Peter's preaching. Starting with this position, they connect salvation with receiving the fullness of the Holy Spirit. This makes the coming of the fullness of the Spirit connected with an initiatory experience of saving grace. Some would like for this to become the paradigm for interpreting the other comings of the Spirit. If this interpretation is followed, Paul's experience is seen as a salvation experience over three days, Cornelius and his household have an initial experience of saving grace, and the Ephesians are coming to salvation in Jesus after having been John's disciples. The filling of the Jerusalem church in Acts 4 would be a refilling of the Spirit for witnessing, and the story of the Samaritans is understood as an exception, with salvation in two stages.

A difficulty with this approach seems to be related to the principle that the clear passages should interpret the unclear. Acts 2:38 itself is an unclear passage. We have already seen at least four possible ways to interpret Peter's invitation and the response of those on that day.

Using the same principle that the clear interprets the unclear, it seems that the best place to start for understanding all the work of the Spirit is the coming of the Spirit in Acts 2:1–4. This is not only the clearest way in which the Spirit is described, but it also has the benefit of the interpretive support of the Gospels that allow us to understand this as an experience for believing disciples of Jesus. If this passage then becomes the paradigm for understanding the others, a proper interpretation of each in the passage looks like this.

The work of the Spirit on the pilgrims at Pentecost (Acts 2:38) should be interpreted as either an initial coming of the Spirit (option two) or their experiencing God's salvation with the fullness of the Spirit coming later (option four). The experience of the Jerusalem church (Acts 4:23–31) could well be the sanctification of some of the three thousand (2:38). The Samaritans have clearly come to an experience of salvation and when the apostles come down, we see the Holy Spirit doing the sanctifying work of God in a second definite act (Acts 8:12–17). Paul then may be understood as experiencing the fullness of God's sanctifying work three days after his experience of encountering Jesus on the road to Damascus (Acts 9:17–18). The Ephesians would be understood as believing disciples with a faulty understanding of both baptism and the Holy Spirit. When those theological issues are straightened out, they can be understood to be candidates for the sanctifying work of the fullness of the Spirit in their lives (Acts 19:1–7).

This interpretation makes the experience of Cornelius and his household in Acts 10 probably the coalescing together of the experiences of salvation and sanctification through the Spirit because of the godly faith of these people (in an Old Testament sense). This experience seems to be the exception, and it is given in order to demonstrate the fullness of what is available under the new covenant for Gentiles as well as for the Hebrews.

What we have been able to do in this chapter is to trace some experiences of God working through His Spirit through an entire book. This involves a larger work of interpretation that is not as easy as dealing with only one passage as we have in most of our other studies. But it is part of the overview that helps us see some patterns for the way God is working. In this case, the overall pattern seems to confirm what we have seen earlier, that God is doing a deeper work in the lives of those who are serious disciples so that He, through His Spirit, might fully control and empower those who are believing Christians.

Prayer Suggestion

Thank you, Father, for the multiple examples of the way you sent your Spirit upon the lives of people in the New Testament church. Thank you that You still make Yourself available to those of us in other ages. Help me to concentrate my attention on the work of the Spirit as making possible a deeper, more intimate relationship with You so that I might live under Your full direction in every area of my life and reflect Your character and thinking in every relationship and act of service for You.

Memory Verses
Acts 4:31, Acts 15:8–9

Additional Passages for Study

You may wish to study some complementary passages during the Word portion of your devotional time.

1. Acts 4:23–37.
Outline this section. Identify the parts of the prayer that led to the infilling of the Spirit and then the results that followed from it.

2. Acts 8:4–25.
Outline the story. What are the comparisons between Simon and the other Samaritans? The contrasts? Can you think of another rebuke in the Gospels that is as strong as the one Peter gives Simon? What was the long term effect of that rebuke?

3. Acts 9:10–19.
Make a list of all the characteristics of Ananias. While the text does not say he was full of the Spirit, what is the evidence that he might have been?

4. Acts 10.
Outline the chapter. What evidence do you find of Peter living in the fullness of the Spirit? What does this story imply about growth after the infilling of the Spirit?

5. Acts 11:19–26.
List all the characteristics of Barnabas. What fruit do you see in his life of being "full of the Holy Spirit"?

The Spirit-filled Life

Stephen: Living in the Spirit

QUICKENING YOUR THINKING:

1. Have you had the privilege of personally knowing a Spirit-filled, mature mother or father in the faith whom God has significantly used in the spiritual lives of others?

_____

2. Would you like to be this kind of person? Do you desire this enough to pay the price to let God make you this sort of person?

_____

✣ GOD'S OBJECTIVES AND THE MEANS TO GET THERE

The basic paradigm of God's objectives and means to achieve them looks like this:

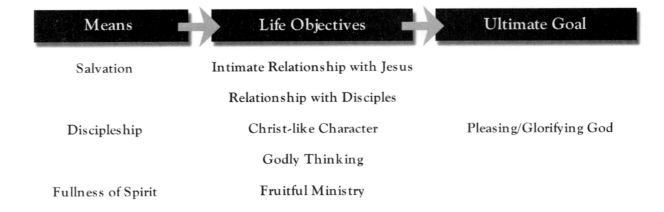

Means	Life Objectives	Ultimate Goal
Salvation	Intimate Relationship with Jesus	
	Relationship with Disciples	
Discipleship	Christ-like Character	Pleasing/Glorifying God
	Godly Thinking	
Fullness of Spirit	Fruitful Ministry	

✣ LIFE OBJECTIVES

The first way (life objective) to please and glorify God is by cultivating an intimate relationship with Him. Then out of this intimacy it is possible for God to work in us to give us a Christ-like character that reflects His own holiness of heart and life. This also makes it possible for God to shape our thinking so that we reflect the mind of Christ. This should be done in close relationship with a few other disciples seeking to know Him in the same way. These relationships, working through our character and thinking, make it possible for

God to work in us to touch other people for Him. Fruitful ministry to others, both public and private, is part of God's design for us.

✛ MEANS TO ACHIEVE OBJECTIVES

The three major ways that God accomplishes these objectives are the means that help us develop and maintain this close relationship with Jesus, out of which all the other objectives flow. The first means is an experience of salvation by grace through faith. The second means is an experience of discipleship through an extended time of life to life sharing, accountability, learning to use the means of grace, and being committed to a band of other like-minded disciples. The third means is the sanctification of disciples through the fullness of the Holy Spirit. [For additional Bible studies on these objectives see Coppedge and Ury, *Knowing Jesus: A Guidebook to Mature Discipleship*, The Barnabas Foundation.]

✛ OBJECTIVES AND MEANS IN THE NEW TESTAMENT

All of these objectives and means are seen in the life and ministry of Jesus and in His training of the twelve. However, the question is, did they get translated to other generations in the early church? Did the twelve effectively pass them on to others? Jesus and what happens with the disciples around Him are one thing, but what about those coming *after* Jesus and the twelve?

It is particularly appropriate to ask this question since we are in the line of those who have not been in the physical presence of Jesus but are still interested in being His disciples. Were the key things about God's purposes and means of accomplishing them through Jesus able to be transferred to other generations of serious disciples?

Part of the answer comes from the lives we see in the early church of people trained by the disciples or by others who had been under the training of the twelve. One of these examples is the life of Stephen. There are several important reasons for the two character studies that Luke gives us in Acts 6–8. One of them is that these two men are not disciples who became apostles. Rather, the stories of Stephen and Philip give us pictures of non-apostolic laypeople who are trained up in the church and become effective for God in significant ways. A key motivation for including these two stories is surely that some of the same things that Jesus is trying to do in the twelve are also accomplished in the lives of many others in the early church. Stephen and Philip become representative examples of what God would like to do in the lives of many, whether it is in the New Testament church or in any future generation.

◆ GOD'S MEANS TO ACCOMPLISH HIS OBJECTIVES IN STEPHEN'S LIFE

If God's objectives are to be accomplished in Stephen's life, what are the things He did to accomplish these objectives? In other words, what are His means to see that His ends (objectives) for Stephen come to pass? We have already noted that there are three of these. Let's look at the evidence for each as it appears in Stephen's life.

Turn in your Bible and read carefully Acts 5:42–7:11, 7:51–8:2.

1. SALVATION BY GRACE THROUGH FAITH

What is the evidence that tells us Stephen has experienced God's grace in salvation?

_____

_____

_____

It is interesting that we do not have the story of Stephen's conversion. This means we do not know when he came into an experience of saving faith, but the evidence is clear that it *has* happened. Without receiving God's grace in this way, no relationship, especially no close relationship, is possible with Jesus. And without this relationship, none of the other objectives God wants to accomplish are possible. So the fact that God has worked in Stephen's life is also part of the evidence that he has come into a right relationship with Jesus through the experience of salvation by grace through faith. This is always the beginning of knowing Jesus and the first step in becoming His disciple.

2. DISCIPLESHIP

The basic means of discipleship can be summarized under the **LAMB Principle**. Where discipleship is taking place, there is always some **L**ife-to-life sharing, some **A**ccountability, the proper use of the **M**eans of Grace, and a context like a **B**and of disciples. Let's look at the evidence in Stephen's life to see in what form these may appear.

▲ Life-to-life Sharing

There are some parts of Stephen's life before he appears on the scene in Acts 6 that we do not know anything about. It would be nice to know that one of the twelve apostles had invested directly in Stephen's life. This is very possible since he was chosen to be a part of the second tier of leadership in the church, but we have no direct evidence to support this. But there are indications that he has learned from some real life models. These models may have been the apostles, or they may have been trained by them. But somebody has modeled for Stephen some key things that he is building into his life.

There are several areas where the apostles were modeling key things that either directly or indirectly have been transferred into Stephen's life. One of these is the close intimacy with Jesus that allows Him to reveal His will for their lives. What do you see in the story to indicate the apostles are living in this close relationship with the Lord?

_____

_____

One indication of this closeness is that Jesus is clearly revealing to them that they are to make prayer and the ministry of the Word priorities in their lives (6:4). Nothing is more productive for intimacy than the privilege of this kind of ministry. Further, in chapter 5 when the Lord speaks to the apostles in prison and charges them to stand in the temple and speak to the people the words of life, they do exactly as they are told (5:20–21). They are hearing from the Lord and doing as He asks. This intimacy with the Lord and the deliberate priority of this in their lives is certainly not lost upon Stephen.

A second area the apostles model is Christ-likeness of character. How does the story in 5:17–42 reveal this character of the apostles?

_____

_____

_____

The boldness of the apostles before the Sanhedrin in chapters 4 and 5 is a clear indication of a willingness to be fully obedient, whatever the cost. The disciples know, like Stephen in chapter 7, that the Sanhedrin certainly has the power to put them to death. Yet they choose to obey the Lord whatever the consequences (5:29), and they count it an honor to be worthy to suffer for the name of Jesus (5:41). They are committed to God and to His truth, just like Jesus, and they reflect the character of the Lord in themselves. This is exactly the character Stephen himself picks up from their model.

Another area the disciples have demonstrated before others is the crucial importance of giving themselves in ministry to others. We see this in their lives from Acts 2–6 in a variety of ways. They are preaching, teaching, dealing with personal spiritual needs, serving others through healing, etc. They are called to serve the Lord, and Stephen certainly picks up this attribute. He has a real servant heart and is willing to do the behind the scenes ministry of distributing bread to the widows. He is also looking for a public ministry of sharing his faith, which leads him to his opportunity for witness in the synagogue (6:9ff).

A quick look at the ministry of the apostles makes it clear from their preaching and teaching that communicating the mind of Christ is centrally important. Where do you see evidence for this in 5:17–42?

_____

_____

_____

Because they focused their ministry upon the teaching of the Word of God, "the Word of God increased; and the number of disciples multiplied greatly in Jerusalem and a great many of the priests were obedient to the faith" (6:7). By more effectively handling the Word of God, tremendous fruit followed.

A further example of thinking the way Jesus thought is in the apostles' use of the principle of multiplication. When they realize they cannot do all the ministry that needs to be done, they propose that others be added to the leadership team to do the work of ministry. This principle of multiplication included Stephen, so he certainly does not miss the lesson that this is God's way of thinking about ministry and the church.

So whether this story includes direct personal investment of the apostles in Stephen or not, there certainly is some modeling that he picks up on and builds into his own life. The sharing of one life with another produces significant fruit in Stephen.

▲ Accountability
What natural context do you see in the story that would provide accountability for Stephen?

_____

_____

Stephen's accountability probably came in the form of the group of seven deacons of which he was a part. Working with them would have been the natural place for this direct accountability to have taken place. There may also be an implied accountability of the seven deacons to the twelve apostles. In this case, the seven would have been serving in some measure under the direct leadership and oversight of the apostles themselves.

In any case, the apostles themselves are modeling for Stephen and the others a principle of accountability. In these chapters you never see an apostle alone in ministry. They are always together in twos or more. There is a built-in accountability from the way Jesus trained them, and this has certainly been passed on to others like Stephen.

▲ Means of Grace

Someone has helped Stephen build into his life the means of grace. These spiritual disciplines that connect us with God and allow His grace to continue to work in our lives are the same group of disciplines that Jesus built into the lives of the twelve (cf. Matt. 4–6). Only the discipline of fasting does not appear on this list.

Under each of the means, see what evidence you can find that these have been incorporated into Stephen's life.

The Word of God_____

_____

Scripture Memory_____

_____

Prayer_____

_____

Public Worship_____

_____

Giving_____

_____

While we are working from narrative literature and therefore do not have a list of the means of grace, it is clear that these key spiritual disciplines have been incorporated into Stephen's life. He is using them to cultivate his relationship with the Lord, to let God work His objectives through him, and to maintain the fullness of the Spirit in his life.

▲ Band of Disciples

It is likely that Stephen would have been part of one of the home groups that received the teaching and preaching of the apostles (5:42). Is there any other evidence he is a part of a small band of other disciples?

_____

_____

The most obvious is that he is serving together with a group of seven whom we often call *deacons* after the Greek word for *service*. The fact that these are chosen to work together in this way is a reflection of the apostles' own training by Jesus within a band themselves.

So the evidence indicates that all the major parts of being a disciple of Jesus show up in Stephen's life. There clearly has been some life modeling for him, he is certainly accountable to some others, the means of grace are working in his life, and he is a part of a group of other serious disciples following the Lord.

▲ The Importance of Discipleship

All parts of the discipleship process (the **LAMB Principle**) are significant in Stephen's life for two reasons. *First, there are the tasks of growing and developing as a disciple of Jesus after his experience of salvation by grace.* He is not saved by doing these good things, but after he experiences redemption by the free grace of God, he then uses these means of discipleship both to maintain and to grow in his relationship to Jesus.

Second, these principles of discipleship also serve him after he experiences the infilling of God's Spirit in full sanctification. These are the tools that allow him to maintain this fullness of the Holy Spirit and also to grow in this deeper experience of God's work in his life. Without these elements built into a disciple's life, it is very difficult, if not impossible, to continue in the experience of the fullness of God's Spirit or to grow in maturity at a deeper level of Christian living. [For further Bible studies on the LAMB Principle of Discipleship see Coppedge and Ury, *Following Jesus: A Guidebook to Mature Discipleship*, The Barnabas Foundation.]

3. THE FULLNESS OF THE SPIRIT

▲ What is Said About Stephen

Repetition in scripture is always a key to emphasis. When an author repeats something more than once, he is saying, "This is very important, pay special attention here!" Observe the emphasis on the Spirit in Acts 6–7 and indicate what is said about Stephen and the Holy Spirit.

_____

_____

_____

_____

If we apply the law of recurrence to this story, apparently the most important thing Luke has to say about Stephen is that he is full of the Holy Spirit! On four different occasions Luke talks about Stephen being full of the Spirit or the Spirit being upon him in an unusual way.

The fact that this is listed as a distinguishing characteristic means that obviously not *every* Christian is full of the Holy Spirit. Yet, this is a condition for serving in a leadership role (6:3). The apostles, having been filled with the Spirit themselves in preparation for ministry, pass along this principle to the next generation. No one is ready for ministry to others who is not fully under the control of the Triune God through the Spirit.

We do not know *when* Stephen was filled with the Spirit. Possibly he was in the group in Acts 4 when they prayed and experienced the full coming of the Spirit (4:31). While we do not know this for certain, what we *do* know is that he was filled with the Holy Spirit. Luke's repeated mention of this does not leave any room for doubt.

▲ Conditions for Being Filled With the Spirit

In addition to the definite asking for this experience, we have seen that there are two basic conditions for a disciple to be filled with the Spirit of Jesus. The first is total self-surrender. What evidence do you see of this in the life of Stephen?

_____

_____

_____

_____

The second key condition to being filled with the Spirit is total trust in Jesus. What do you see in the story that indicates this is true of Stephen?

_____

_____

_____

The question for us as contemporary disciples is, are both of these things true in our lives? Does the Spirit have you in the same way that He had Stephen? Are you full of the Spirit of Jesus in the same way that he was?

◆ THE EFFECTS OF BEING FILLED WITH THE SPIRIT

1. A CLOSE PERSONAL RELATIONSHIP WITH JESUS

Go back through the passage and indicate what evidence you find that Stephen lived with an intimate relationship with Jesus.

_____

_____

_____

2. RELATIONSHIP WITH OTHER DISCIPLES

Review the evidence that Stephen had a close relationship with a small group of other disciples.

_____

_____

_____

3. CHRIST-LIKE CHARACTER

What are the indicators that you see in these passages that Stephen had let God develop in him the character of Jesus (i.e., the character of the Holy Spirit)?

_____

_____

_____

4. GODLY THINKING

Looking at the whole of Acts 6–7. What evidence is there that Stephen had developed the mind of God and was thinking as God thinks?

_____

_____

_____

5. FRUITFUL MINISTRY

What does the data reveal about the kinds of ministry that Stephen had?

_____

_____

_____

_____

_____

_____

✥ THE WHOLE PICTURE

When the Spirit comes in His fullness, there are some remarkable results. There is a deeper intimacy with the Triune God when the Spirit of God has all of a person. This is clearly illustrated in the life of Stephen. He knows the Lord intimately and well, and he is wholly His. This is particularly evident in his dying moments as he looks to Jesus in the midst of hostility and stoning (7:55–60).

There is also bonding together with other disciples. When the Spirit takes full control, He removes the self-centeredness that keeps us from being close to other people. There are some godly men who are bound together in spirit with Stephen and are deeply grieved when he is taken from them (8:2).

There is a definite likeness to Jesus that comes from the Spirit's fullness. Stephen must certainly be one of the clearest examples of Christ-likeness of character in his own life. His prayer for the Lord to "not hold this sin against them" (7:60) is strikingly parallel to the plea of Jesus on the cross, "Father, forgive them, for they know not what they do" (Luke 23:34). This is certainly not a natural reaction! It is a supernatural reaction that comes only by the transforming power of the Holy Spirit that makes us like the person of Jesus. It happened in Stephen's life!

The Spirit's coming upon Stephen certainly is responsible for the bringing to his mind the scriptural truth he shares with the Sanhedrin as a model of godly thinking (Acts 7). This is the longest discourse in the New Testament on Old Testament theology and history, and it comes from a laymen whose primary job is not the ministry of the Word! But he has soaked himself in the Word, sat under the ministry of the Word, and has had the Spirit quicken the Word to his own thinking. This means the Spirit is able to bring this to the forefront when it is necessary for Stephen to share these truths before the Jewish leaders. Not only is he sharing truth, but he is applying it to their circumstance in a remarkable way.

The last result of the Spirit's fullness is an empowerment for ministry. Stephen has the power to serve in a background ministry where there is very little credit. He has the power to witness in the synagogue of the Freedmen. It is so effective that "they could not withstand the wisdom and the Spirit from which he spoke" (6:10). He has the power to speak boldly before the Sanhedrin (7:2ff), and he is obviously used of the Spirit to impact Saul of Tarsus in the moment of his death (8:1). Whether in a service ministry or a speaking ministry, there is clearly an empowerment to do the things Jesus and the disciples did. The power does not come from Stephen but from the Holy Spirit.

As you come to the close of this study, thank the Lord for the provision of His means. Ask Him to indicate to you whether or not there is one or more of these means that is not as fully built into your life as they were into Stephen's life. Whatever He says, you want to respond to Him with a fresh commitment to that means so that He might accomplish all His objectives in your life.

Memory Verses
Acts 6:3–4, 10.

Passages for Additional Study

You may wish to study some complementary passages during the Word portion of your devotional time.

1. Acts 21–22
What evidence can you find for the Life Objectives/Goal in Paul's life in these chapters?

2. Acts 10:1–11:18
What evidence do you see of the Life Objectives/Goal in Peter's life?

3. Acts 8:4–40
What evidence do you see of the Life Objectives/Goal in Philip's life?

4. Daniel 1, 3, 5, 6
How do Daniel and his three friends demonstrate the Life Objectives/Goal?

Further Bible Study

Where do you go from here? Having successfully completed this workbook, the obvious question is, What do I do next? If you have found these Bible studies helpful, let us suggest some other studies which will aid your continued growth.

The Barnabas Foundation is a discipleship-training ministry that has a strong desire to provide resources to help serious disciples mature in their walk with Jesus. To help with the training of disciples and to assist growing disciples in their spiritual lives, we have produced some additional guided Bible studies, much like the pattern you have been using in this workbook. These are our suggestions for further digging into the Word:

Knowing Jesus: A Guidebook for Mature Discipleship

This set of Bible studies focuses on Jesus' five *life objectives* for His disciples and His ultimate goal for them. If Jesus is training disciples, what does He want to see happen in their lives? These studies walk through the Gospels to assist you in discerning what His purposes are for those who are following after Him.

Following Jesus: A Guidebook for Mature Discipleship

These Bible studies are on the major *means* of following Jesus as a disciple. They include studies on life-to-life sharing, the central role of accountability, the use of spiritual habit patterns (means of grace) that cultivate one's walk with the Lord, and the vital significance of being part of a group of disciples.

Serving Jesus: A Guidebook for Mature Discipleship

How do you move as a disciple of Jesus to *becoming a disciple-maker*? These Bible studies guide you through Jesus' pattern for disciple-making as you prepare yourself to be involved with Him in making other disciples.

A Workbook on Spiritual Gifts

How do you understand the role of spiritual gifts in the life of a disciple? This set of Bible studies focuses on the three major gift passages in the New Testament and shows how they relate to each other. They include a guided study for determining your own basic giftedness so you can see more adequately how you contribute to the Body of Christ.

A Word about Barnabas Foundation

The Barnabas Foundation is a discipleship training ministry with a vision of fulfilling the Great Commission in every generation. Its mission is to train and encourage disciples, disciple-makers, and spiritual leaders.

To accomplish this mission, the Foundation provides:

1. DISCIPLESHIP-TRAINING EXPERIENCES FOR:
- Students in colleges and seminaries
- Laity in local congregations
- Spiritual leaders in conferences, seminars, and continuing-education events
- To assist in this disciple-making process, Barnabas teams provide discipleship training seminars for local churches, education institutions, and leadership events

2. THEOLOGICAL AND PRACTICAL RESOURCES FOR DISCIPLESHIP:
These include guided Bible studies such as this workbook and the following directed studies:
- *Knowing Jesus*
- *Following Jesus*
- *Serving Jesus*
- *A Workbook on Spiritual Gifts*

The Foundation has also produced some *Key Idea Books* for thinking disciples. These are short books that challenge serious disciples over important ideas from scripture. Among those available are:

- *God's Purposes for You*
- *Setting the Pace: The Life and Ministry of John the Baptist*
- *The Promise of Something More: What Happens after Three Years of Discipleship With Jesus*
- *When the Holy Spirit Comes: What are the Results of Being Filled with the Holy Spirit*

The Barnabas Foundation is also producing *The Timothy Letter* as a short challenge to contemporary disciples. It is available free of charge by writing to the Barnabas Foundation at the address below.

3. A NETWORK FOR THE ENCOURAGEMENT OF DISCIPLES THROUGH:
- Teams available for seminars, retreats, conferences, and revivals in local churches and on the mission field
- Conferencing of spiritual leaders in the United States and with missionaries and national leaders around the world

For further information on how the ministries of the Barnabas Foundation may assist you, your group, and your church, please contact:

The Barnabas Foundation, Inc.
P.O. Box 200
Wilmore, KY 40390
(859) 858-0099
e-mail disciple@barnabasfnd.org
www.barnabasfnd.org